Tails Of A Social Worker

by
Carol Sue Barrett

Order this book online at www.trafford.com
or email orders@trafford.com

Most Trafford titles are also available at major online book retailers.

Printed in the United States of America.

ISBN: 978-1-4269-7088-7 (sc)
ISBN: 978-1-4269-7089-4 (e)

Library of Congress Control Number: 2011908484

Trafford rev. 06/08/2011

 www.trafford.com

North America & International
toll-free: 1 888 232 4444 (USA & Canada)
phone: 250 383 6864 ♦ fax: 812 355 4082

To Mom and Dad,
and to Byron, my son.

Acknowledgements

Thanks to my dedicated friends who encouraged me to write this book. Last but not least, this wouldn't be possible if it weren't for God's help.

Isn't the word misspelled? Isn't the word spelled t-a-l-e-s? No, it's able to be spelled both ways. The story tells many tales. Its characters all have tails. Only animals act this way. Their instinct is to kill. They act on their instincts without conscience. The various tails and tales will come into play throughout the book.

Table of Contents

Prologue

TASHA
TASHA had a need,
Could not concede
Not knowing where life would lead
From her gentle heart others would feed.

TASHA grew cold and bold;
Vowed never to fold no matter what insensitive traits life
  showed.

She often bent – but never broke
In and out a dream she would float.
Educated, emancipated, beautiful and tough,
Dealing in the system these things were not enough.

TASHA walked the line fulltime
TASHA struggled without a dime
Could not slow down;
There was no time.

Consolation she could not find
Nothing it seemed brought peace of mind.

TASHA married, TASHA tried.
TASHA maintained her need inside.
She suffered the hurt in this hell of a home.
TASHA broke free, she started to roam.

Perverted educators all respected by their names
Lusted after TASHA but she would not play their games.
They guaranteed her good grades and gratitude delights,
TASHA would warm their waiting beds occasionally at night.

TASHA wept, could not sleep.
Now and then you need a friend,
Sometimes you can't relate to kin –
TASHA on her own again.

By Your Cuz

* * *

A Social Worker is defined by Webster's Dictionary as: "Any of various professional services, activities, or methods concretely concerned with the investigation, treatment, and material aid of the economically underprivileged and the socially maladjusted." N.A.S.W. is the abbreviation for the National Association of Social Workers. This is the official umbrella that all colleges and universities receive their accreditation through. In other words, neither the student nor the institution will be taking their courses in pursuit of a degree in Social Work in vain. In order for any academic institution of higher learning to offer degrees in Social Work; N.A.S.W. (National Association of Social Work) must approve that curriculum. I joined N.A.S.W. while attending St. Louis University on the Undergraduate level. Students got discounted rates for joining. Once you become a graduate you had to pay more. Being that I went from Undergraduate to Graduate school, I was able to enjoy the student discount rate for some time. The fee went from a mere $35.00 annual membership to $85.00. As a professional Social Worker you can afford to pay the fee. After all this was what I had burned all the midnight oil for all of those years. I couldn't wait to get my first job and sign my name with the official M.S.W. written behind the name of Tasha Chelsea Barebones, M.S.W. My first job was working as a Social Worker for the Jefferson-Cass Health Center's Maternal and Infant Care Project. The Jefferson-Cass Clinic was very important to me for two reasons. Being that I was a teenage mother myself and my son was born on a nearby street. 2737 Madison Street was located a mere two blocks away filled my heart with glee. As a matter of fact it was the Social Workers at this very site that influenced me to go further than high school for me and my son. Lynn and Yoly were the two Social Workers who brought me school bulletins to prepare me for academic pursuits.

I've been out of high school for at least six years and I'm afraid I won't be able to do as well as I did in high school. All in all it was a struggle at first. I began to take courses at night at the Forest Park Junior College. I did this for six years taking two courses each semester - working all day, going to school at night. I began taking English Composition at first, along with a course in American History. I loved History anyway. I loved English, so naturally I received an A in both. I knew that Grade Point Averages were very important, so I wanted to get as many A's on my official transcripts as possible. I was serious about wanting to excel in school. I had heard such bad things about going to a Junior College that I was really afraid. I heard that they were smoking Marijuana all over the campus. I heard that the instructors were not capable to teach. I also heard that they didn't give a damn about what you learn because after all it's just a Junior College. All of the proceeding sentences were incorrect. I must truthfully say that my instructors were terrific. I must say that I encountered some very good lectures and they could care less about your family or your non-academic pressures. All they wanted to do was make you learn their subject matter. They expected you to do well on their examinations. If you were having problems understanding any of the materials being taught the teachers were available for individualized sessions to assist you. There was no need for one to fail. One thing was difficult for me. I had no friends to socialize with. I knew no students. My classmates had long been out of college. After all, I had one goal in mind to keep a 3.5 average so I could be accepted at either Washington University's School of Social Work or St. Louis University School of Social Work. I had to keep this in mind at all times no matter how many years it would take for me to get enough credits to earn my Associates Degree in Liberal Arts. Finally the day came. I had to sacrifice my income from the Jefferson-Cass Health Center. If I planned to finish a one year course of study within one year, I had to quit work and carry the 12 hour course load each semester. At last I had to resort to going on A.F.D.C.

(Aid to Families With Dependent Children). I had to also apply for Food Stamps. I'd never been on the Welfare Rolls in my entire life. I could remember how Mother resented hearing the word A.D.C. (Aid for Dependent Children) when I was a child. Here I am applying and then eligible for such a program. Again, my primary concern was going to school full time until I was able to obtain the Master's Degree in Social Work. One thing that I kept in my mind was that I'd be accepted for who I was and what I was. I felt that once I completed school, men would not attempt to want me to go to bed with them so quickly. They'd respect me. They wouldn't disrespect me. Was I in for a rude awakening to real life in the world of Social Work. No school had prepared me for sexual innuendos, sexual harassment and outright black balling from your profession when you'd reject their sexual advances. Was it true that not many Blacks excel to high posts when they are fighters for their clients or their co-workers?

In reality, the answers to the above questions became very clear. I began to work very closely with the National Federation of Federal Employees, Local 1431. I was the editor the Sentinel Newspaper. The Sentinel Newspaper was the official labor newspaper for the East Orange Veterans Medical Center, East Orange, NJ. My job as editor was for me to print events regarding legislation for Civil Service Employees located at job sites in this region of the country. I also served as an elected official for the union. I was 1st Vice President and Lobbyist. Mr. West became very uncomfortable with me being that involved with the labor union. He didn't encourage me. On many an event scheduled for out of town he denied me paid leave to attend the function. After all, he was a member of the Management Team. Was this the real reason behind his frustration with me? It wouldn't be that I was experiencing discrimination as a Black Female from my service chief. After all, he's a married Black Male, his wife is a professional woman; and he has at least two daughters. I'm sure he wouldn't indulge in such behavior. He was also from St. Louis, Missouri. That's how I learned about him as a fellow "homie". I mean by the term "homie" a person who previously lived in the same hometown as me. I had worked or entered the United States Civil Service system as a GS-9 from the Register in St. Louis, Missouri. I accepted a position as Social Worker at the GS-9 Level at the Kansas City, Missouri Veterans Administration Medical Center. Our staff was so closely knitted. One of my close colleagues in the Social Service Department was pretty and smart. It was here that I began to see what female Social Workers experienced. One thing was prominent. All of the females were basically unmarried. The men or male Social Workers were married. Our Service Chief of the Kansas City Veterans Hospital was a Black Male also. The staff was predominately White. Mr. Gooden was highly respected throughout the hospital. The department of Social Work was highly respected. No one was talked about as rumors, tales or gossip pieces. I was so proud of my new job. I was actually selected over three other candidates for the same position. One of the candidates that I was competing with for the same position I knew well from Graduate School. He finally accepted another position at another VA Hospital in California. My tenure at the Kansas City Veterans Hospital was basically great. Until this day, I still communicate with some of the staff that I formed close alliances with. One of my childhood pals from grade school lives in that town and works as a Claims Examiner Supervisor with the Social Security Administration. I'm very close to all of my friends. Once I've made you my friend, you're my friend for life. I guess that's why my telephone bills stay so high. They stay in the status of disruption of service. I can't imagine life without being able to pick up the phone and call St. Louis, or South Carolina at least whenever the need to talk to someone for support is necessary. Another thing is very important to understand. Once one enters working for the United States Government they usually remain there until they retire. They receive a yearly evaluation and salary increase. Social Work as a profession is generally as a rule of thumb overworked and underpaid. That's the reason U.S. Government Social Workers eat crap, get sick and retire from the same station. One works diligently in school looking forward to living out that dream of helping clients to change their lives and looking forward to the first paycheck. In the last year of Graduate School, your dream becomes real. You're then told if you will receive your diploma. Well, I'd like to know why this issue hadn't been brought up earlier in academic studies. Anyway, I'd rather get out and help someone like they helped me. Besides, I have all of this financial aid to repay. By the way, how do I expect to ever repay these loans when my salary is so low? I attempted to explain this to the Regional Department of Higher Learning Student Loans Division and they told me that I should have gone into education. Those graduates who majored in education and were willing to be assigned to teach in a rural or poor urban areas would get their student loans reduced in payment greatly for two years. Medical students also received this. What a shame for me to find this out after four years. My old car had to be replaced with one that runs. I was helped to purchase a new Chevrolet. It was nice, a brand new sky blue Monte Carlo with a Landau top. Now I could get back and forth to work. My car enabled me to feel good about myself and get to work to make the payments. When I drove to my new job in Kansas City, Missouri, I had a new car. We went to many an affair after work on the Alameda Plaza in K.C. "The plaza" was so pretty at Christmas time. It was all decorated with Christmas lights. Each and every building on the plaza was decorated. Don't mention Crown Center. It looked like Fantasy Land. I wanted to move to New Jersey so I could be near to my sisters. My mother and father also lived in New Jersey. I've always loved New York City. I liked the New Jersey shore. Nature was so beautiful to see near the ocean. When the ocean roared, the waves would come into shore. The ocean air had a smell that existed nowhere else except near the shore. I'd telephone Mr. West often to inquire about my transfer to New Jersey. Each month, I'd make the call. I kept Mr. Gooden informed of my steps (red tape) in the transfer. As soon as I was transferred, he had replaced me with someone else.

Finally, the day came. I cried at the thought of leaving Mr. Gooden and the staff. I asked Mr. Gooden if he thought it was a good idea to transfer to the East Coast. His reply was you'll have to adjust, but I like the West Coast. His goal was to move to Seattle, Washington. He and his wife invited the entire staff over to his house in attempts to offering a degree of hospitality to all. When I finally had to move, I had many a farewell party given in my honor. Yes, I'd miss Kansas City.

I'd heard of the military type of atmosphere that existed in the Veterans Hospitals. I'd heard that the VA was merely an extension of the Army. Women who were employed as professionals were treated as second class citizens. Some of the men both staff and patients resented women in any type of position of authority. In many instances the patient or staff member was reported to the next person in rank. Patients who interacted in a highly negative manner were reported to their physician. The incident was discussed in Team Meeting. The patient was always given priority. His behavior was overlooked in many instances because of his illness or his age. Staff would often times be confronted on an individual basis. If it couldn't be resolved on an individual basis, the issue would be discussed with one's supervisor. As I'm involved in explaining the bureaucratic system to you, I'm also laying the groundwork for my case of sexual harassment and deformation of character against the East Orange New Jersey Veterans Administration Medical Center. The Equal Employment Opportunity Commission case was being filed on the basis of the Tort Act. The Tort Act is a wrongful act for which a civil action can be initiated. My experiences at East Orange Veterans Hospital will be explained to you as you read this book, that is why I had to file a Civil Action Suit against the VA Medical Center.

Chapter I:

SEXY WOMAN

I was the sexiest woman in the Midwest, west of the Mississippi River that just happened to be St. Louis, Missouri.

On January 25, 1970, I returned to work after maxi-facial surgery and was told by my supervisor that I was a seductive woman. I was informed by my new supervisor that I was to have a conference with him for pre-evaluation of job performance. The yearly performance evaluation was not until May. Strange, I thought, this isn't anywhere near the spring. Anyway, the evaluation (excuse me) the pre-evaluation conference began. It was quite obvious that he was not able to evaluate me in that he was preparing himself five months in advance. He, also, had to rely on my ex-supervisor's evaluation of previous years as a means of guidance. My ex-supervisor was female. The existence of a personality clash would interfere with an objective evaluation. That lady and I were close to the same age; she feared I would have an affair with her lover, who happened to be my co-worker and colleague. Her opinion had a great deal of influence on my new supervisor. This lady was divorced, and parented two children. Here I was divorced, and alone. My son was an adult and a sailor in the U.S. Navy. He and his wife lived in Florida. I had no mortgage or home repairs to maintain.

As a matter of fact, I was place on a "L.W.O.P." (Leave Without Pay) status while relocating from St. Louis, Missouri to New Jersey due to selling my home prior to final relocation. To fly from St. Louis to Newark amounted to large sums of money if done frequently enough. Instead of having the time charged to my vacation I had to get no money at all. Here I was a professional employee facing this kind of opposition prior to the move and long drive here.

Once here I met my new supervisor in person. I most certainly didn't feel welcomed. Actually the director of that department made the transfer possible. The lady was merely doing what she was to do by job description - orientating the new employee to this office. Boy, had I made a mistake I thought. I had to remain under this lady's supervision for three years. I worked an "Irregular Tour of Duty" during that three year span. The tour hours were 1:00 P.M. until 10:00 P.M. Monday, Tuesday and Wednesday, Thursday hours were 8:00 A.M. to 4:30 P.M. I had regular days off at least - Friday and Saturday. Every Sunday I worked from 9:30 A.M. to 6:00 P.M.

For at least two years, I wrote letters asking for at least one Sunday a month off. I was denied for three years. It finally came to the point of disliking the position. But I refused to quit. I began concentrating on having a flaw in my face corrected. This began in the Summer of 1968 culminating with maxi-facial surgery on October 13, 1970. All of these things came back into my mind while listening to this newly appointed supervisor telling me that I couldn't be evaluated because I was seductive. Another co-worker resigned, oh excuse me, he retired. This employee had worked at least 30 years at this office. He, also, advised this worker he needed psycho-therapy. As a matter of fact, this individual removed himself from being a supervisor to being the all too familiar psycho-therapist. He was quite impressed with himself. He was not able to handle this newly gained authority. He held individual conferences with each employee as a way of getting to know each other. "A way of establishing trust on a one-to-one basis," as he called it.

Instead of getting to know and establishing a degree of trust, each worker was told that to keep their jobs, they would have to take psycho-therapy. I'm speaking of practicing professionals with ten to thirty years of practice after getting a Master's degree. I'm speaking of people with life's experiences that newly appointed supervisor had not achieved yet. We became enraged. We met our director and he told us that this guy was "laying out the Gospel". We all needed to be shaken up. He was chosen for the position over three other highly qualified individuals. We were all certain that he, of all people, would not be appointed to that position.

Speaking of favoritism, well here it is. Hungry for power, power making one act out all of his dissatisfaction with himself? Yes, I'd have to say yes. A little power has gone to one's head. A little power eats at one and one's desires to destroy all that he comes in contact with, be he worker or supervisor. This person told me that my work was unacceptable. I should not work anymore until I took psycho-therapy. My behavior was viewed by my supervisors and my co-workers as seductive. After all, he only saw me as seductive. He told me that he had been in psycho-therapy four times. It had helped him tremendously. He encouraged me to take the therapy under his therapist. By now I was in tears. My surgery was not six weeks old yet. I believe that when an individual acts this way, he has an under riding problem himself. You know it all came out in the wash. He was of minority descent. He was angry with his mother and never resolved this conflict.

My rebuttal included an official memorandum to him and his supervisor. Blind copies were circulated to the Departmental Human Service Director and the Labor Union. The case should have gone to the Office of the Equal Employment Opportunities Commission for a hearing on sexual harassment. Instead I was advised to file a grievance. I began filing but stopped because the Director advised me that I would have a new supervisor. Pressure had been brought on my department due to the blind copies of the original letter of complaint. In the end, I was evaluated and given "Marginal Level of Job Performance". I could have been terminated due to such an inferior rating. I was, of course, unable to get any raise that year and I couldn't get a job promotion. I attempted to change careers and was denied job change. I had to wait for my performance evaluation the following year.

My newly assigned supervisor was Mr. Leonard Saberstein. Mr. Saberstein warned me on our very first conference that if I had any objections to anything do not write about it, let him know. He voiced his objection to the blind copied memos. My union representative of the department was Mr. Gustav. Mr. Gustav sat with me in an unannounced conference called by the department director in response to my letter of protest of my being called a "Seductive Woman". There was a meeting being held between management, the department director, my immediate supervisor, and my newly assigned supervisor. My right to fair representation was going to be violated had my union representative not been with me. The department director was upset with my colleague who was my union representative. My new supervisor was announced and he became unable to control himself. He asked my labor representative to leave. He both asked why Mr. Gustav was in this meeting and then asked Mr. Gustav to leave in the same sentence. Mr. Gustav was very polite and looked at me and asked me if I would be "ok". I assured him that I'd be able to deal with my new supervisor since as of this day the issues were being resolved once and for all.

"At least that was why the meeting was being held," I thought. Before Mr. Gustav left the room though he made a statement as to why he was at the meeting. He replied, "Tasha invited me to attend, that's why I'm here." He then gathered his belongings consisting of a union contract book and his pen and pad. You see, Mr. Gustav wasn't considered as one of the favorites. He was known to be very outspoken on issues that were what appeared to be unfair towards staff also. The director then commented that he wanted the issue to end regarding the "Seductive Woman".

They had no idea that the president of the agency had copies of the memorandum and that the issue would reappear. I thought this meeting was in response to those blind copied memorandums.

The first vice-president finally called the department director into his office and asked him to give him the facts surrounding the memorandum. He also asked for the way in which the issue was resolved. The Department Director then became an enraged devil.

I was then caught walking outside the office near the Employee's Cafeteria on the fifth floor. The devil pointed his finger in my face. He stood about 5'6" tall. He had the slightly bald head with "cow-licks" as my mother called it a marked faced.

His lips were thin and his eyes protruded more when he became angry. While pointing his finger in my face he said, "You want my job, don't you? You won't be around to get it because I'm going to fire you! You don't write up this department's business and spread it all over the agency." I was then unable to eat, my stomach knotted up and I broke out in sweats. The minute I returned to my office, I told my union representative what had just happened.

He assured me that this guy does this to anyone that makes him angry. He tried to calm me down. I was upset indeed. My new supervisor Mr. Saberstein then called me to his office for a meeting. The meeting was very brief. He drew a chart of the chain of command better known as the pecking order, or the line of protocol.

The honeymoon period with the new supervisor was fun. It only lasted until the end of Summer. He'd take a group of us on walks for lunch. This would help us lose weight. We all began to smile at our new figures. The group consisted of 5. We actually hated for fall to come. Fall would cause us to end our daily walks. Fall was the time for us to think of returning to school to further advance ourselves in the upward ability realm.

We'd have what was called continuing education classes at the job site. These classes were taught by college professors to keep us in touch with what was being taught in the classroom. Lo and behold the sessions were being held on "Sexual Surrogates." Sex surrogates are very popular in this region of the country. The professor was well versed in teaching individuals to become surrogates. Teaching was done by showing films depicting one in the various positions of having sex with quadriplegics or paraplegics. The agency was East Orange Veterans Hospital, located in East Orange, New Jersey. The hospital treated veterans both in the hospital and on an outpatient basis in the clinics. We referred them to community services also.

It so happened that a lot of our patients were afflicted with gun shot wounds. They were involved in various types of freak accidents that left them paralyzed from the spinal column down. The lower extremities were paralyzed; they were helpless. These could be either males or females. We actually had more males. The film therefore depicted females as the sex surrogates. These women were actually paid to give these patients sexual gratification by whatever means. Sex surrogates used oral gratification which includes taking their tongue and kissing the client or patient in the face or mouth, or running their tongues alongside the body in the hopes of reaching a sensitive spot of arousal. Those who suffer spinal cord injury are generally unable to use their body from the neck down or from the waist down. That means that these individual have to have a very good and loving partner or spouse. If these individuals don't have either then they may turn to the sex surrogate for imaginary or real gratification. In other words, men do not get an erection , women are not naturally stimulated either. Can you imagine life without sex?

In some instances the women had to pick the patient up out of the wheelchair to assist him to the bed, to assist him to remove his clothing. Orgasm was done by what appeared to be epileptic seizures, or severe tremors. In many instances also just hugging, or holding and being massaged by an elbow or hand was the male or female patient's form of orgasm. In the female patient who was quadriplegic or paraplegic, she too had to use imagination when it came to breast stimulation or clitoral stimulation. Just the touch of a human being meant so much to these individuals.

By half-way through the films, it became obvious by Continuing Education Class #2 that my male colleagues were experiencing difficulty in maintaining their professionalism. They had begun to have problems in keeping themselves in a non-erected state.

Some of the men were seen with erections. Even Mr. Saberstein became red in the face. I could hear all kinds of remarks being made around me, I could hear groans also. The purpose of this segment of classes was to help us to counsel the couple, individual or patient group who had suffered and endured such a tragedy. Instead the guys were taking out their inability to handle the films on me. I was asked why I wouldn't consider taking classes to become not the Social Worker but the sex surrogate instead. After these three sessions on this subject ended the continuing education department asked us for an evaluation of the course. Do you know that these people were unable to evaluate the course? These people really caused me to be unhappy.

I had already been told I was seen as seductive. Well who is fooling who? I was then told that I'd make a good surrogate by the continuing education coordinator. I needed to take psycho-therapy because I am seductive. I then became self-conscious. Was it really me who was causing all of this unusual interaction from everyone? I would come to work for these classes on my off days. Mr. Saberstein told me that I was dressing improperly. I'd wear warm-up suits on my off-day and my colleagues saw the warm-up suit as seductive. I was told anytime I'd step into the building be it off-day or not I was to be dressed as if I were coming to work. Besides, the warm-up suit was too revealing. During the movie, I was informed by Mr. Saberstein that my colleagues were watching me instead of the movies on sexual surrogates. Winter came and here it was springtime again. I was then given another clinic area to work in. I was in charge of chart rounds. The areas assigned were orthopedics and rehabilitation medicine. It was really challenging. Discharging meant making sure the patients were hooked up or assigned a caseworker at the Welfare, Food Stamps, Rental Assistance or Social Security Office. I also was responsible for keeping accurate chart notes on each client.

Statistics were vital to us being funded. Each month we all had to complete our statistical reports. There were many nurses who had been in the orthopedics clinic for 10 through 15 years.

These women became permanent fixtures in that clinic. They actually got to know patients/clients that were what is called chronic patients. They knew a lot of things about each one. Since they were in the clinic so long that meant that they could not, they would not accept any new ideas or concepts. Anyone that didn't agree with them would make them feel uneasy. Their role was to get rid of that individual. The older nurses made it difficult for the new nurse to do her job. The new nurse and I became good friends plus we worked well together in dealing with our problem patients. Those were patients who wouldn't keep their clinic appointments or take their medicine. The charge nurse was Puerto-Rican. It was difficult to understand her English but she managed to do the job very well. All was going well for me and the nurse. As a matter of fact I had excelled in getting along with staff and patients but this was short-lived. The older nurses became jealous. All of a sudden patients became unhappy. Families began to complain about the least trivial things. How long did the patient have to wait to see the doctor? Why wouldn't the patient wait until the doctor wanted him to wait for his cast to come off his leg?

The head nurse saw the various means of sabotaging at the meetings. For example the 19

doctor would be in the operating room at the time of the team meetings performing an unexpected emergency operation. The doctors wouldn't answer their beepers when I would page them, or they would go to lunch at the time of the meetings. You name it; all in the name of upsetting me, the new Social Worker. The new nurse became upset.' She had a little boy that was 3 years old who lived in Puerto Rico with her mother so she decided to move back to reunite with her family. Another nurse was quickly assigned the position since none of the older nurses wanted the position. Why should they? They were comfortable in their jobs. They acted together only to keep up confusion. A new nurse began. Friendliness was only her mask. This nurse acted so nice but she wasn't nice too long. My new supervisor Mr. Saberstein would meet her for lunch and take her to meetings that I wasn't included in. All of a sudden I began to notice no team meetings at all being held.

Team meetings for the rehabilitation medicine clinic ran good. The chief of that service was aware of the need for team meetings. He therefore, cooperated by insisting that his staff attend the meetings. There was one nurse who was devious. She was white and tall and thin. She acted as if she was working with me then I found out she was working against me. This nurse constantly called down messages to the office demanding to see me immediately when I'd go to the area she'd explain the situation which was nothing like she explained on the referral note.

There was one black R.N. on the floor named Mrs. Christian. Mrs. Christian had very pretty smooth cold black skin. She was about 5'6" tall ready to retire, she always told me, but it didn't register because she looked so good. Mrs. Christian called me in the kitchen to tell me that my new supervisor would come to the patients' charts and go through the records and take out my recordings. Amidst her cigarette smoking she'd notice from the kitchen area what he was doing. He felt as if no one would tell me what was going on because he had no idea of whom I associated with. Mrs. Christian assisted me from her post by letting me know when patients needed me. Everyone, including the patients, was suspicious of this guy.

This guy's scheme was finally revealed to me. He and the new nurse in orthopedics, along with the doctors wrote a letter to the Director of Social Work asking that I be demoted from being a Social Worker on that service. As an issue in focus they asked that I not be allowed to practice in that clinic. My job should be limited to answering the telephone only. To add insult to injury I had just recently returned from a ten day suspension without pay. My rent was behind. I had just returned to work from the surgery earlier that year. I was taking bio-feedback sessions from my oral surgeon for fear of facial disfiguration.

I could either resign now or await my termination. The ten day suspension was excessive in view of the reason for the suspension. It was strange. I was suspended because I falsified records. Wouldn't you think I knew better? You bet I knew better than to falsify records. Tasha had committed a crime. She must pay for her crime. We'll hit her below the belt. We want her to quit working here anyway. I'm sure she'll get the message. The least little thing that she does will make her eligible to be terminated. We will get her to quit. I didn't tell anyone about my suspension. I attempted to appeal it but the labor union wouldn't assist. I was told by the president of the labor union that I needed to take psycho-therapy because my priorities were out of focus. This obese lady who looked like Porky Pig asked me to agree to take psycho-therapy. She told me that the only way that I could avoid getting terminated was to take psycho-therapy. I had never been told that I needed psychotherapy before by any other job. As a matter of fact I worked part-time while attending graduate school. In addition to working I was raising my teenage son alone. Anyway I found out that the suspension would continue no matter what I would do to stop it from occurring. Social workers were viewed by the various other administrative departments in a very negative sense. It was common knowledge of all the sexual covert and overt activities of Social Workers at this hospital Husbands were leaving their wives because of their outside flings with their counterparts (fellow Social Workers). One good looking Social Worker had impregnated his supervisor while dating another female Social Worker at the same time. As a matter of fact, sexual activity was common in this hospital amongst social work staff. They would pick out whom they wanted me to have sex with. I had already chosen my partner not to their liking. I was the odd ball because I'd tell them I wasn't going along with their choosing.

The head of the department of social work dictated to all of the female and male workers in a very unorthodox way. He had all of them afraid. He'd threaten them with telling them he made it possible for them to live good lives. I felt bad about working for such a negative unit. I along with some other workers decided amidst my problems to have a Recognition Day for Social Workers. Finally, I told everyone about my impending suspension. While I was on suspension without pay, I began looking for work. The recognition day was successful. The turnout was good.

People came from various agencies and hospitals in the area. Well, to be honest I was so hurt I was ready to cry. I bought a new blouse to wear with my navy blue wool skirt. The blouse had a white satin sailor type collar. A light blue satin bow tie made it stand out. We all purchased our individual corsages. Quite a few of our colleagues did not participate in the event because they knew that the whole event made our department look like hypocrites.

I left work that day and headed for the famous bar in East Orange where all the black bourgeois hung out. The music selection was all jazz. They prepared hot h'or d'oeurves trays for you to meet and greet friends both old and new. It was a gathering place to allow one to be able to say "Thank God It's Friday", TGIF day. I met a new friend. He'd actually just experienced the same type of incidences on his last job. He was an accountant for a large pharmaceutical firm. We became good friends. We'd talk often on the phone to each other. He gave me a shoulder to cry on. I'd call him at least once weekly. One day I was dialing his telephone number and dialed a number similar to his.

Anyway, I dialed the wrong number and asked for him. I began talking to him as if he were my intended party. The conversation went like this: Hello John. The party answered no this isn't John but I'll be John if you want me to be. If you've got time you can talk to this John. You're not 367-1234. No, I'm 377-1234. The party then asked me my name. I then asked him his name. We both exchanged our correct telephone numbers. We tried to figure out where we lived. Well, what the heck. This voice sounded so intelligent. He didn't sound like a psycho or weirdo.

I felt safe in giving him my correct name and telephone number.

Well John called back. We were arranging a date. We both attempted to describe ourselves to each other. The telephone conversation went like this: Say, where is a place where it's safe for both of us to meet? I want to see you. Oh, I want to see you too. Oh, let's meet at the World Trade Center where the Path train stops. I'll meet you at the Telephone Booths. We'll meet at 5:00 P.M. I then became scared. This guy is nuts. Why do we have to meet in New York? After all I live in New Jersey. Yeah, but I'll be getting off from work in the city. It's more convenient for us and safe the voice stated. Anyway, I cancelled our meeting. He telephoned the next day. I then asked him where he worked. He was a mechanic at a large international trucking company. We then both decided that I'd feel safer meeting at a local place in Jersey. I choose a neighborhood diner that I frequented as I knew people who knew me. We then described each other's cars and exchanged license plate numbers. I was looking at myself in the mirror making sure I looked my best. All of a sudden I looked at the rearview mirror and began to smile with approval at my blind date. We then were looking at each other face to face. Besides, he had such a beautiful smile. His skin was a beautiful brown. His skin was clear, he wore a nice moustache and medium length side burns. He was dressed the way I like New York guys to dress. He wore a beautiful suede jacket, a dark blue turtleneck sweater, a pair of blue wool slacks, a pair of blue slip-ons. Man, he looked good... He carried a red rose and as I finally removed the keys turning the motor off he handed me the rose. After all I thought about waiting across the street to make sure he wasn't a weirdo with horns or tails. Instead we said, "Hi". "I'm John, and you're Tasha". He was at least 5'9" tall. He weighed about 165 lbs. We held hands and went inside of the diner. It was a well known Diner located in Irvington, New Jersey. Well, as you might guess breakfast lasted every bit of two hours. We merely ate pancakes, scrambled eggs with cheese and sausage. This place was/is noted for its ability to attract a multi-ethnic crowd of customers because of the variety in its daily menu. He kept wanting to know the reason that I got suspended. But as he put it throughout our conversation, "I'd like to add happiness to your suspension instead of you going through depression." That's exactly what he did starting with that day. We began by leaving the diner and going in our own individual cars to a very nice wooded area called South Mountain Reservation in South Orange, New Jersey. We took a long walk through the trails designated for walking. It was a nice clear sunny day.

We became best friends. He constantly called. Our means of communicating became our "telephone recorders". He had so many different messages. I'd attempt to copy his style of messages and it became just good clean fun. Our dates were infrequent because of his hours of work and the distance he traveled to work but all in all we remained best friends. Were we lovers or were we platonic friends? Well, you can love someone without ever becoming sexually intimate. Besides, he was the same age as my son. I had a lot of trouble with dating men in my own age. Generally my dates were younger. But John was special. He'll always be.

Well, April came and went. I was constantly putting up with my new supervisor's lies, abstractions, distractions and deceptions. He even walked with me and two other co-workers each day for exercise.

Well, May 22nd is my birthday. When my birthday arrived, I was so caught up in my job that I didn't enjoy it. However, my boyfriend from New York City, Harlem to be exact; made me enjoy his birthday and mine. He took me to Atlantic City to enjoy one hell of a show. May 30th weekend it was Jacques and me. I returned to work the Monday after the holiday to be called into my supervisor's office. I was then advised that I had written enough letters to EEOC. These guys were angry. They got the Personnel Department Office involved. These three guys all banded together to make me feel all alone. From 2:00 PM - 4:00 PM, I sat with them the day after the holiday. I was asked to resign from my job. I told them that I wasn't willing to resign. They then told me that I had a bad track record. They told me that I talked too much. My business was everybody's business. Social Work business was everybody's business. The next day, I again was told not to go to my office but come to the Director's office. I was in this office two days consecutively. From 8:00 AM - 12:00 noon, I was told to quit or I'd be fired. They'd really meant for me to quit. They had gotten letters to the fact stating that I needed to be taken away from working as a Social Worker. The Doctor's decided that I had begun to abuse patients. Mr. Saberstein told me that the wheels were in motion and they couldn't be stopped. I was told that he hadn't ever been mentioned in an EEOC case before. He didn't like it. By then I noticed that I had begun to feel faint. I had begun to have sharp pains in my chest. I began to break out in sweats. I managed to walk to Employee's Health with another supervisor's help. She actually did whatever the big boss told her to do. As a matter of fact, speaking of being a seductive woman - she was it. She was the one who wore Splits up the sides of her Skirts, or the Vest without a Blouse;;– she looked decent ..sexy body.!! She was either scared that I would have a Heart Attack or she was helping our boss out. I was examined by the Employee Health Physician. I was sent home with another co-worker.

My Oral Surgeon had monitored me closely throughout my recovery. He felt that I had done exceptionally well. All of a sudden, I began to suffer with High Blood Pressure, rapid Heart beat and finally Duodenal Ulcers. As I walked up the steps to my apartment building, I noticed that the stairwell and everything that I saw had now turned black. The hallways were black because I was sick. I went to my Doctor's Office. He was tall man, Six Feet tall at least. He reminded me of my father in the way in which he was built. He was of Italian descent. He is very well known throughout the Medical Field. If he couldn't perform the test himself for the various illnesses, he'd have the specialist come into his office to do the procedure. I told my Doctor, who I liked so much, of the predicament at work. He was appalled. My good friend Linda gave me the name of the attorney who was also upset with the various ways in which I was harassed. My colleague and good friend Melvin Gustav would call me each day to see how I was getting along. He also offered to lend me money if needed. He would tell me to remain strong. He told me, "Tasha, I never knew anyone before that has actually gone through the extensive humiliation that you've gone through. Tasha, one thing, you should have never quit your job." Another colleague Larry said in joining in with Melvin, "You never quit your job, leave your man, or get put out of home be it your house or your apartment."

Larry said, "Tasha, fight for those three things." All of these things came into my mind as I was in an ambulance going to the hospital. I had begun to experience internal bleeding. I had no idea that I was bleeding. I knew I was weak, my heart was beating fast. Besides, I'm not sick. Everyone had begun to look at me and ask me how I felt but I was functioning as a Social Worker. Although the ten day suspension without pay had left me in a state of worry, I still held on.

I had also started going to church on a weekly basis. The choir sounded good. The minister reminded me of my Daddy. This was around Easter when I began to attend church on a weekly basis and the Crucifix was the topic of the Sermons. I finally joined church. The church was located on the same street that mother and daddy lived on before he retired. They stayed there for at least fifteen years. My girlfriend that invited me to this church had often times invited me and I'd always say, "I'm coming to church with you, Arlene." She was so shocked and happy when I joined. I joined a Baptist church. I needed faith. It looked as if my very means of existence was being snatched away. My minister visited me in the hospital. The church sent flowers and money. I felt that God was with me. The real estate office then sent me a notice to appear in Landlord Tenant Court. The bills had fallen behind. My doctor kept me sedated for the first four days of my two week stay in the hospital. I had money in the retirement system which amounted to approximately $10,000. I signed for that money to be forwarded to me but only after I repaid the credit union. I had to borrow constantly to pay my oral surgeon, the orthodontist, and the dentist who did the extensive cosmetic work of caps and crowns. How was I going to survive?

The Labor Union of which I was a high ranking official in print only, did nothing to fight on my behalf. Not only had I been called a Seductive Woman, told that I needed psycho-therapy by both my immediate Supervisor and Deparartment Administration but the President of the Labor Union agreed with them. I was very tired of all of this insanity. I was the Lobbyist, Vice-President, and Editor of the Newspaper. Although I had resigned from my position at the hospital, I was still asked to run for office. Instead I resigned. It was clear that the Union wasn't about to offer assistance. I filed an EEOC (Equal Employment Opportunity Commission Complaint) instead. These guys were really upset. My troubles increased. I was told to quit or be terminated. Both the head of the department, my supervisor and a Personnel Specialist told me the same thing, at the same time, in the same room. Besides, my supervisor told me that I had been chosen to be fired. The firing was due to all of the infractions caused by myself in the area of Interpersonal Relations. There was an alleged List of Patients that I had Abused and also Neglecedt on the number of occurrences this year. The massive Dental Corrective Surgery last year, my having to take Bio-Feedback Theapy two times per week at $70.00 a session and here I am being coerced to resign!!. Where was one's right coming into play? I am the Lobbyist for the Medical Center, I am the First Vice-President of the Labor Union and the Editor of the Labor Newspaper. I had been called a Seductive Woman and a Provocative Woman, which really hurt me greatly. If I am Seductive or Provocative Woman, what does that have to do with my Job Performance? The Labor Union proved to be an organ in existence minus what it's philosophy is based upon. The Labor Union had combined with Management against me. The President of the Union told me to take Psycho-Therapy because if I didn't drop the EEOC complaint of Sexual Harassment I'd be sorry. She told me that I had no idea of the predicament that I was placing myself in. You want to know something funny, the president of the Labor Union had retired at least ten years ago. In her vain attempts to persuade me to drop the case she advised that I couldn't have a case against the Suspension and EEOC going simultaneously. She was wrong. These were two separate issues. I became sickl throughout all of these things going on at once. In addition I was going to work each and every day. The Stress had far excelled me being aware of it. My Heart had begun to beat faster and faster. I had begun to break out in Sweats without any forewarning. I began to feel uneasy at any Departmental Meetings because everyone was aware of the problems between my supervisor, the Department Head and me. To my surprise, I had begun internal bleeding. My Doctor looked at me and told me that I was being admitted to the Hospital. I had no idea that I was that ill. I was hospitalized for fourteen days. I had just joined church in the early part of the year. The church was called Mt. Olive Baptist of Newark, New Jersey. My parents lived down the street from the church before Daddy retired from Amtrak Railroad Company. Mother was in her prime during those days. She was driving me wherever I wanted to go. She still refused to believe that I was grown amidst her caring for her Eight Year Old Grandchild Byron. She still wanted to know who I was going out with. She would fear me loving New York City so much. She knew that I'd be out all night long in the Jazz Nightclubs, etc. She'd love to hear about my adventures. She and Daddy were Seventh - Day Adventist, so she had left "worldly pleasures" a long time ago. It made her face light up with joy when I'd tell her what Jazz Musician played during the show.

She'd beg me to attend Sabbath Services with she and Daddy. "Ok mom". I'd give in but I knew that I could never be a member of this denomination again. Mom cried because she thought that my soul was lost forever to the non-affiliation of the Seventh Day Adventist Church.

During my hospitalization, I reflected on all of these things after the first four days of absolute bed confinement, IV Fluids, and Heparin Bag had been removed. I was told that I was at Death's Door. The Bleeding was so severe. I was put on a Bland Diet, and I was told not to return to that job.

Mr. West and Mr. Saberstein had already forced me to resign before the hospitalization. I attempted to rescind the resignation, but they refused to acknowledge it. They were too happy to get me to that point. They weren't about to allow me to change my mind. Although they were aware of my hospitalization they continued badgering me at home by sending letters demanding that I remove my personal items from my office. They also wrote me a letter advising that they were holding my Final Paycheck until I cleared my valuables from the office. At this point my lawyer intervened. He asked for the Department Head and relayed to me that he couldn't believe that this guy was a Department Head. He told me that he thought the Department Head Mr. West sounded like an ex-Mental Patient. I told my Lawyer that everyone is aware that the Executive does have a Mental, or either an Alcohol or Drug, Problem.

Anyway, the letters of harassment stopped. Can you imagine not being able to get a good night's sleep for at least one and one halve year? All of a sudden after hospitalization you are now given a list of foods to eat and foods to avoid. Alcohol is no longer able to be enjoyed. To have a Duodenal Ulcer that has ruptured is like having an open wound that's in the process of healing. You must keep the wound dry and clean in order for it to heal properly. I had no one to depend upon for support except myself. What was I going to do? A friend came and took me home from the hospital. I then realized that my Rent was now two months behind. Late charges were Three Dollars per day after the Fifteenth of the month. I had no way of paying my rent.

The suspension also threw me behind and now the current Hospitalization Bills, my Charge Accounts, all added up and were still being charged interest. Don't mention Student Loans. What am I going to do? After all my Doctor and my Lawyer were aware of my circumstances. They told me to try not to let these things worry me. I was able to take Librium nightly, which caused me to sleep without waking up seeing all of these things which prevented me from sleeping. The minister was very supportive along with the Senior Choir and Church Members. My name was placed on the Prayer List. Only God kept me alive and kept me with a roof over my head. The next day at the Unemployment Office in Irvington, New Jersey I stood. I was so weak. I was there early. I was so humiliated. I had never been unemployed in my entire life. There were at least six different forms to fill out. You take your Social Security Card and your last Payroll Stub and stand in line. "What am I doing here anyway?" I looked at the various people in line who were getting their benefits extended because they were Chronically Unemployed due to their occupations. I also looked at the ones who bragged about lying in the sun in Jamaica or Puerto Rico while having their checks mailed to their home. They were back home merely to obtain the next two weeks benefits and go somewhere else for fun. Then there were the serious individuals like myself whose main priorities were to obtain a job so that one could resume their normal way of life.

I went through the Unemployment Job Referral Bank and met a very good counselor who kept me informed of positions in my field. I also used the New York Times and the Star Ledger Newspapers throughout the summer. I must have mailed at least Seventy Five Resumes. I can see writing the cover letters and the envelope, and including the Resume in each instance. I had gone on many a Job Interview in New Jersey to no avail. It was as if someone had put out a bad omen against me because I couldn't get hired on any job that was anywhere near my previous position at the Medical Center. Had I been "black balled"? Something was going on. I finally landed a job at the Child Protection Services Bureau. Well I took a Ten Thousand Dollar Salary Cut. At least it was a steady income. I felt so low in this position. You were a glorified Babysitter and a "Policeman of the Parent". Your job was to make Unannounced Visits on a monthly basis to each name on your Case Load. If you had Thirty Open Cases, that meant you had two days each week of Working in the Field to do Home Visits. My ages ranged from Birth to Ten Years Old. My Caseload consisted of working with Youngsters who were in Permanent Foster Care who t were removed without Parental Consent. In some cases the child's life was in danger due to the Parent's Neglect or Parent's Abuse. I never attempted to work for this agency before and hopefully I'll never have to do it again. Most of the Supervisors don't hold a Graduate Degree. They basically hold Bachelor Degrees. Many of the Caseworkers only hold High School Diplomas. I was perceived by many as being a threat because I held an Associate, Bachelor and Masters Degrees in Social Work. One's day isn't a normal Nine to Five. Your day consists of working until Twelve O'clock Midnight or maybe until One or Three O'clock AM in the morning. You are to be at work at Nine O'clock AM the next day. You are to log all your overtime and you must have your Superior's Approval before you can use your Overtime. The cars that we were to use for Field Assignments were overall new cars. After taking children to the Doctor's Office, to the Hospital Emergency Room, or going to the school to talk to various School Officials about a Child's Behavior minus your Lunch or Dinner saw the car being used as your Table. The children had to be fed in many cases because they missed their meals. The car oftentimes was dirty inside. Many times the foster parent became angry when the caseworkers were unable to give them a Voucher to purchase a new mattress or new shoes for the child or children. They were given a Clothing Allowance and a Medicaid Hospital Insurance Card which entitled the child to have his/her prescription filled and have their doctor's visit paid for by the state also. .. The Child Protection Bureau Caseworker staff has a number of Caseworkers that practiced Alternative Lifestyles. Some of them were unable to separate Work from Home. One of the most Adorable Caseworkers was killed by his Partner.. The office was shocked because he was such a nice person. His supervisor and he got along quite well. The Caseworker's Supervisor was one who was very vindictive. If you made a general statement that injured her frail ego, she never would forget. This woman was so powerful that she ran the district officer manager's role. He was the puppet...When she pulled the string and he'd follow her command. I obviously had to be informed in that I was the new kid on the block. I listened well to my informant. We actually became very close. They had demoted her because she wouldn't go along with the Politics of the System. They were allowing her to regain her old position back. This time she had promised to play the politics correctly. Meaning play our way, not your way. This is not Burger King' you can't have it your way. One of the Supervisors whom most Clients and Co-Workers hated was the supervisor who was instrumental in getting me terminated. As a matter of fact, "This is not Burger King, you can't have it your way" was posted on her wall. She never knew how to speak in a low voice tone. Each time she attempted to speak it would be so loud that the whole office knew that she was talking. She was approximately Five Feet tall. She weighed at least Two Hundred Twenty pounds. She had big breasts that looked like they were size 40D. She was a fair skinned Black Female who had worked her way up from lowly Caseworker, Investigator who had answered severe cases of Child Abuse and Neglect to Divisional Supervisor. Her best friend was a White Female Supervisor. As a matter of fact both of them had the same first names "Susan". When you called one, you'd have both of them answer at the same time. They both possessed dispositions that were similar. Nasty! How could these people call themselves child care workers? They'd sit around after office hours bragging about how many cases they'd done that were truly horror stories. One case involved an African family. The family moved to New Jersey twelve years ago with four children. One child was retarded. He had a set of triplets as his younger siblings. The Father spoke English fluently. He didn't allow his wife to go to school to learn English at all. The wife was so overwhelmed and so dependent upon her husband that she always followed his commands. The Husband realized that he was unable to provide adequately for all eight of his children plus himself and his Wife. According to Susan, he left the children on many occasions with no food.

The children were actually starving to death. After at least ten Unannounced Visits it was Documented that the children were Malnourished. It was found that the family was also here illegally. Not only had he broken the Immigration Law but he was also endangering the life of each of his children. According to Susan his rationale was that children don't work for their food so they can't eat. The case was then referred to the Court for Removal of the Children. My job was to get the Father to agree to let his Wife take English As A Second Language Classes. This would hopefully allow both of them to agree to Psycho-Therapy on a Weekly Basis.. The Plan of Action., was for the Parents Visitations bi-weekly at the office of Children's Protective Services with me monitoring the entire visit. These children were very unruly. The parents would cook their Ethnic Dishes for them. The Playroom that was used for Family Visits became a room filled with garbage, strewn about with broken toys and soiled dishes. Invariably, the parent's dishes would upset the children's stomachs. When the children returned to their Foster Parents' Homes, the Foster Parents would call me the next day to ask that the parents cease this practice. The Father kept asking me when would he get his children returned to him. I'd ask my Supervisor and she'd always recite the manner in which the children were found some four years ago. I asked her did she consider the possibility that sometimes people change? Of course, I was being insubordinate.

Another case involved a child that reminded me of myself. Her eyes were big and brown. Her skin was a beautiful coconut chocolate color. Her mother had Sexually Abused her, her Eldest Sister and her Younger Brother. The Foster Mother who had been caring for her at least four years experienced her Husband Sexually Abusing another couple of Foster Children in that home. This child began to scream out of windows. She'd masturbate anytime or anywhere. It seemed as if she'd stop crying or experiencing emotional trauma when she masturbated. Her Biological Mother used bottles in the girl's Vagina. The one boy experienced a bottle in his Anus. Of course, the mother was using Alcohol and Drugs. She had experienced these things herself as a child.

The Paternal Grandmother wanted the children to live with her in California. The plan was for me to take the children there by Airplane. They were to have arrived the week of Christmas. The Bureaucratic Red tape was at least Twenty-Five different forms and /procedures. The children could not leave until each step had been signed and countersigned. I had to find out the cheapest way of getting to San Francisco, California. The grandmother would have met me and the children at the airport. Everything had been finalized. I'd spend five days in San Francisco and return to work the following Monday. "No, Tasha. It can't go like that," said 'Les. You'll have to take the children there and return back on the next flight. I looked at her without thinking. My reply was "No. How can you all expect me to do this to my body? Do you really mean that besides getting the children from their foster mother's home, getting the baggage into the car, driving to the airport that I'm to then fly to San Francisco and return back on the next flight?" The answer was "Yes. You are to return on the next flight." I then told my immediate supervisor who acted like a child of the new change of events regarding the case. She then telephoned the grandmother in California to inform her that the children would have to have their trip delayed. The grandmother became enraged. Finally, I telephoned her to tell her the entire story. She finally decided to pay her mother, the children's Great Grandmother to fly with them since I couldn't. Well the Great Grandmother agreed to take the children to California. The morning of departure finally arrived. The Biological Mother who had been missing all of this time was actually awaiting my arrival in the office that day. The Great Grandmother had contacted the mother to inform her of what was going on with her children. The Mother hugged her children and kissed them goodbye at the airport. As soon as they all were home in California, the Grandmother called to thank me. The Biological Mother hasn't contacted me since.

I began to get attached to some of the children. Each case was alike and yet different. One common thread was that they had all been removed from the home for various reasons of Abuse or Neglect. The parents either agreed and did a voluntary placement or didn't agree and the children were removed by a Family Court Order.

I finally began to learn some of the Rules and Regulations in the Department of Children's Services when I noticed that my supervisor began to do like the one at the veteran's hospital. Each day, I noticed Handwritten or Typewritten Notes from her. I was still in the process of looking for other work. I knew I couldn't stay here for two years. I decided to attempt to get my Doctorate Degree in Social Work. Why did I do that? All hell broke loose. During the Admission Procedure to Washington University I was advised of my non-acceptance. I was told by the Director of Admissions that the Department Executive of Social Work had written a letter stating my inability to conceptualize, to perceive or to communicate in any comprehensive manner. I was both appalled and shocked. Enough had been enough. I immediately went to the Office of Equal Employment Opportunities Commission and filed another complaint on these two guys, my ex-supervisor and his supervisor. They were continuing to "Black Ball" me. They were continuing to spread tales that were outright lies.

A sexy woman is a person that feels like she's sexy. She's sexy only with those she chooses to have sex with. You can't force her to have sex and think that she'll change in her attitude towards you. It's like you guys. If you don't want a woman, she can't force herself on you. It must be a mutually agreed upon situation.

I've merely meet a lot of guys at work and not at work who feel that I'm an "easy lay". Well have they been shocked to reality. Guys are now subjected to Sexual Harassment by their Female Superiors. Such was the case with my beach pals Robert and Kenneth. Kenneth and Robert told me that they both had Female Supervisors. Both told of how their Supervisors would entice them in Sexual Acts by having them come into their office and sit with their legs parted in a suggestive manner. One even wore a Garter Belt and exposed that to Kenneth on a warm summer day. Kenneth was raised in South Jersey so he detested such acts. Finally he noticed his position as Book-Keeper Accountant with this large New York based firm was becoming intolerable.

The next thing he observed was a letter in his mailbox advising him that his services were no longer needed. He was terminated. I encouraged him to file an EEOC (Equal Employment Opportunity Complaint) but he refused. Our other pal Robert was a big truck salesman with an international firm. He was doing quite well. He was sexually harassed at his job also and dismissed. You should see how polished and refined these guys look. They'd make any woman want to be with them. Girls have desires too you know.

Sometimes we can't have what we want either. We can't force another human being to do anything they don't want to do. The summer was so much fun. We hung out at Sandy Hook and Belmar Beach. One day we drove all the way down to Ocean City. Robert was hired by another trucking firm for more money, Kenneth and I took salary cuts. We were not accustomed to being unemployed.

Buppies was the place to meet and greet the Buppies from either New York or New Jersey. They all used this place as the gathering spot. Only beautiful people visited this place. It appeared that way. Under the soft lights with non-stop jazz music playing, sometimes a live band, who wouldn't enjoy going there. Basically, I wasn't a bar person. It is something nice that attracted me to this place or in downtown Newark on Fridays directly after work. I'd switch either the place in East Orange or this one but I'd keep a regular seat at this bar. I'd make sure my make-up would be placed on to perfection early that morning before going to work. At Five O'clock PM, I was on my way to Boogies or Buppies.

Jacques was met at Boogies. He is my good friend who was stuck by me throughout the crisis. He was actually sitting in my chair when I met him. He lives in New York City. We look so good together. He is built like an Atlas. He's very smart.

He's at least ten years younger than me. We've talked about the age differential especially since he's only three years older than my son. I've actually come to find out that this is the latest trend, younger men and older women. We've danced all night long at various discos around New York City. I've danced so hard that my legs have actually ached. After we get through dancing, he'd say, "Your place or mine?" We never know which place. I've lived in the same place for six years; a studio apartment in Irvington, New Jersey. My neighbors and I are very close. I've seen plenty people come and go and I'm still in my studio. However, Jacques brought a new luxury condo. I actually spend my weekends at his place. He's a lover, friend and companion. It seemed to us that on the nights we'd spend together the "disc-jockey" on the radio would know it. The love songs were so beautiful and many times we'd record ourselves making love on cassette tape. We'd play the tape back and smile and try to remember what we were doing on that part of the tape. His expression was that we poured our brains out on the tape. We sounded so good that we felt that some movie producer or studio recording company could use our sounds of lovemaking as background music. Anyway we went on and on.

My girlfriend, Jasmine is and has been a very supportive friend. We both would complain about our boyfriend to each other. She was truly a "fashion statement". She is at least 5'9" tall. Her looks are so striking. Her skin is so smooth and black. Her mouth is very small and her eyes set apart like an African princess. She walks so tall and statuesque. She's traveled the world over many times. I was so glad to see her again. She'd just gotten back from Africa. We exchanged telephone numbers. I told her of what happened to me and my job and she wasn't shocked. She told me of a similar incidence that had just happened to one of her college room-mates.

I became very depressed. I began to have a milkshake each day. After all I couldn't drink a beer or have a glass of wine due to my duodenal ulcer. My diet was bland. The food was awful. I was the one who visited and ate at the many different restaurants in the village in New York City. You name the restaurant and I had eaten there with my boyfriend or either with a group of friends. The Village along with hanging out at Washington Square Park became my other favorite thing that summer. Jasmine began to call me each day. She'd also go through the New York Times and the Newark Star Ledger newspapers to help me find work. At summer's end that year, she had a few of her affluent friends in her backyard for a combination barbeque and house party. This really reminded me of those days' at home in good ole' St. Louis. Yard parties were plentiful. At least I'd come to meet more folk that could help me do some networking for jobs. I had explained to Jasmine on many an occasion that I felt that I was being "black balled". I had been on many job interviews. The employers sounded as if I'd been chosen for the position of Social Worker. They'd taken me to my future office, tell me the salary, my days of work. All of a sudden I'd notice that I'd never hear from them again. Jasmine refused to believe that an ex-employer would actually tamper with my future in this way. It was real to me. Jasmine would say to me, Tasha they would be crazy to do such a thing. They could be sued for liability". I kept searching for a Lawyer to represent me in what had become a nightmare. I'd gone to at least twenty different Law Firms. It was clear that I had definitely suffered Sexual Harassment by being told that I was a Seductive Woman needing to take Psycho-Therapy to learn Behavior Modification. This is what led to the whole tale of the "Sexy Woman" or a "Seductive Woman". This is what has led into the Tails, or Tales of a Social Worker.

By now the whole department was afraid of our most prominent administrator. Everyone throughout the region had become familiar with his behavior. If anyone would see him they'd readily see that all he thought about was tales, tails, and more tales to tell. In short the guy was nuts. He'd actually ran more good Social Workers away that would cause one to question why? What's wrong? Are you a member of the Clique of Social Workers? To be a member of the clique you have to be accepted by them. The rules to belong were very simple. You tell them your life story. You ask them to give you advice about your personal life. They inevitably would betray your trust and tell your secret to another colleague. It wasn't unusual for them to "swap partners". So you're married. What does that mean? Man isn't supposed to be faithful to his Wife. The Wife is to be faithful to her Husband. Tasha– don't you see you don't belong here? You don't fit into the clique. You're not going to do as you're told. After all, Mr. West' s words were, "Why don't you behave?" I'd asked him what he meant.? He'd tell me to act like the rest of the Social Workers. If I'd behave, I'd find myself obtaining promotions and less hassles. "Dogs behave, Mr. West, because they have to be trained. Some of their tails are short, some of their tails are long, some are curled and some are straight. Hey, I'm going to quit when I'm ready."

Dunkin Donuts began to be my kitchen. After all I couldn't eat normally. I didn't have money to buy Groceries. I wasn't eligible for Food Stamps. My Daily Menu consisted of Soup and Bread and Butter. The people would come to know me and started telling me of their problems. One day this guy was sitting near the window at Dunkin Donuts. He was talking with two other men. One of the men tried to keep my attention diverted towards himself. I noticed someone else. He looked at me and asked me what was I doing sitting in this place. I told him that I was unemployed and had been placed on a bland diet. To make a long story short at this point not to reiterate; I explained my predicament. He began telling me about his sick and elderly mother who lived in Massachusetts. This guy is very interesting. I don't know anyone that lives in Massachusetts. I thought he must come from a well-off family to be from Massachusetts. "Well sir, it's been nice talking to you. I have to go now. I'm running late for an appointment." "Aren't we going to exchange telephone numbers?" "Mister, where is the Mrs.?," I replied. "Mrs. has been buried for at least ten years," was his reply. I noticed his wedding band of solid gold. I still didn't accept that answer. I asked him who he lived with. He again answered, "I live alone". We exchanged telephone numbers. The next day at eight O'clock AM my telephone rang. It was Herman. "Will you have breakfast with me?" "Yes," I replied. While eating out at this nice restaurant in Secaucus, I was told by Herman that he was going to catch my rent up for me. I said, "No, you can't, you don't know me." One thing he said that let me know that he was sent by God to me at that moment. He only hoped someone would help his daughter out if she were in a situation similar to mine. He said that every dog will have his day to wag his tail. He attempted to refer me to, strangely enough, the same attorney that I ultimately used. He kept in touch with me and paid Two Thousand Dollars in back rent for me. The Realty Agent was amazed and nasty in her interaction. Anyway, she had to give the receipt for payment to Herman. I knew that Herman was God sent.

All of these things hurt me so badly. They have left me devastated. They have made me strong. I know that miracles are possible. I know that all things are possible if you have Faith in God and believe that it will happen.

The only way I can keep my sanity is to write. From crying all night, the thought came to me to write a book about some of these events that don't seem possible. From the pain of being called the seductive woman to internalizing that pain, came the idea of writing about Tales/Tails of a Social Worker. The tales are great and so are the tales that they tell. All of us have tails.

Readers: stop and think. Go back and try to remember those moments that you were put in the position of being a Sex Object; or told that you were sexy and you had no intention of playing that game. This could be you. Could you adjust if your co-workers or boss said that you were something you were not? Do you think you could live with it?

The American Heritage and Webster Dictionaries define the word seductiveness as:

1. To lead a person away from duty or proper conduct; entice into a wrongful behavior, corrupt.
2. To seduce to have sexual intercourse.
3. To entice or beguile into a desired state or position.
4. To win over, to attract.

This is a game that you and your group of friends can play. The answers are assigned a numerical rank (i.e., Often - 10; Sometimes - 5; and Never - 0). Anything over 30 or above say that the person is seductive.

1. Do men and women feel you're sexy?
    Often (10)   Sometimes (5)   Never (0)
2. Do you feel that you are sexy?
    Often (10)   Sometimes (5)   Never (0)
3. Do you buy clothes that have intentions of attracting the opposite sex?
    Often (10)   Sometimes (5)   Never (0)

4. Does your cleaner tell you that your scent is sexy that "he/she knows your clothing is in the bunch to be cleaned?

        Often (10)   Sometimes (5) Never (0)

5. Are you invited to parties or on dates as a way of getting to know others?

        Often (10)   Sometimes (5) Never (0)

50 _____

40 _____

30 _____ SEDUCTIVE

20 _____

10 _____

Did you truly evaluate yourself? Did you lie about it? Did some questions make you feel uncomfortable? Did some make you feel good about yourself? What about that man/lady over there? What about your husband, or your supervisor or even your boss, or people you come in contact with (i.e., your pastor, your church sisters and brothers, church elders). What about your school teachers or your doctors? What about the milkman, the mailman, the fireman at the neighborhood firehouse. Is this what life is all about?

Being brought up in the church or from a religious standpoint, one should not have sex before marriage.

Being the first child meant a lot to me. I was the role model of the family. My sisters and I were taught to treat our fellowman as we wanted to be treated. We were to treat all men right and to follow the rules of the Seventh Day Adventist Church, that meant refraining from sex. Well, I resented this. Falling in love included sex. I admit that I had a complex. People called me names because my teeth protruded from my upper and lower lips. I was known by such names as Bugs Bunny, Foot Sue (because I walked with a wide stride.)

My childhood was horrible. Teenage years were not any better. They were worse because of the menstruation period which caused me to suffer with constant pain each month. I wanted to be a Drum Majorette or a Modern Interpretative Dancer but I could not be either. Both were against my religious upbringing. My parents were Seventh Day Adventist and I could not support myself so being that I was a child I had to follow their advice.

But, I said wait; wait until I'm grown. I'm going to do everything I always wanted to do but could not. If I wanted to have sex I could have it when I wanted to; and with who ever I wanted to. I could be the Drum Major, the Flag Twirler or even the Modern Dancer. I could even dress the way I wanted to. I could express my body language through my clothes which I could never wear as a Seventh Day Adventist at home. I could now wear make-up, fingernail polish and jewelry.

People view/viewed me as a sex symbol because my body measurements are 36-26-38 at middle age which causes me to be a plus.

Throughout my life I always believed that anything I wanted to achieve I could because I am a dreamer and a possibility thinker. You see, if I saw the dream; the dream did come true. My son was born at home as a teenager. I knew that I could not depend on my mother and father to support me because I divorced my son's father after three years of marriage. I rejected my son for a while because his father hurt me and prevented me from being a loving and caring mother. My mother and father were there to provide the support that was needed. For this, I am grateful and this is something that I will never forget.

Chapter II

MY YOUNGER YEARS

My first job was working as an executive secretary for the Jewish Welfare Agency of St. Louis, Missouri. I graduated from Charles Sumner High School. During that time, I fell in love and conceived. I was prohibited from participating in my own high school graduation ceremonies. I was determined to go further - I knew there would be other ceremonies that I would participate in.

Where did those four years go? They seemed to have flown by. Here we were ready to be adults, ready for college, or ready to be parents. Those races at the Auto Drag Strips which meant cars going from 55 to 100 miles per hour were gone. You were not in violation of traffic laws on the Drag Strip. This was an area set aside for "Hot Roders". Of course, the guy with the loudest muffler on his car always had more dates than the guy with a nice quiet car. Funny, I've always liked the guy who came from a prestigious family with a loud muffler on his car.

Then there was the guy with his motorcycle. Did I love to see the Black Leather Jackets, the Brown or Black Leather Boots, the tight blue jeans and me on the bike. I thought I was "Miss It".

This meant that I dated guys who didn't live in my new neighborhood. They came from the "West End" or "The Ville" areas. However, all in all, the guys in the neighborhood didn't pick fights. I'd have to say that my sisters were stabilizers because they dated guys from the neighborhood.

The telephone lines stayed busy - three girls with one phone, plus a party line. This was horrible. While you're talking to your date, someone would begin to dial on your call. Sometimes this prevented my date from calling to say he was on his way. All of a sudden, I'd hear a loud muffler being raced. I'd tell Mother and Daddy "Goodnight".

Double Dating was the thing to do. It was a way of getting to stay out later than the time Mother and Dad said to come in. Our boyfriends would take us to White Castle Hamburger stands where the Cheeseburger sold for Five Cents. The waitress would serve you in the car. This was often times Saturday Night Date. The Mississippi River was, also, a popular spot for young lovers to visit. The Gateway Arch was not built yet. My best girlfriend became pregnant at fifteen years old. You know I believe the conception may have taken place on one of our Double Dates down on the Old Mississippi River. The couple married and moved to California. He could take care of a family - he was a High School Senior who worked as an Auto Mechanic during and after high school. This hurt because we had so much fun together. We would attend Drive-In Movies and eat Pizzas. Our favorite movies were "Picnic" and "Love Is A Many Splendid Thing". We would cuddle up to our boyfriends and go through all of the romantic scenes. I looked for that kind of love. I became close to two other girlfriends after my friends moved to California.

Grandmother Susie stayed on the third floor and she'd come downstairs to our house on the first floor. She would come with her Lucky Strikes Cigarettes and her nice pretty low cut dress. She worked as a Maid in the Suburbs.. It was Grandmother Susie who insisted that our English be perfect. Grandmother Susie told mother to take Linda and me out of the Seventh Day Adventist Church Elementary School. These girls need to know how to read and write.

I'd love to spend Saturday night at Grandmother Susie's place. My sister, Linda, spent Saturdays at Grandmother Nannie's. Of our Grandmothers, one was widowed and the other one was separated. We saw both of them dating. Grandmother Susie was my Maternal Grandmother, Grandmother Nannie was our Paternal Grandmother. Actually Daddy's Mother, Nannie and his Father were separated. Daddy would take us to see his Father, Clyde. Clyde was a Maintenance Man for an Elegant Apartment complex in the Ville area. Today that same area is a slum area. Grandmother Nannie was drawing Social Security Checks and working at least two days a week basically to get out of the house. Grandmother Susie was the darker skinned of the two. Her skin was as soft as cotton and cold black. She had a beautifully shaped body and Arthritis that caused her trouble in her left knee. Grandmother Nannie was fair-skinned with pretty wavy hair. She was built nice but she wasn't built like Grandma Susie. I was Grandmother Susie's favorite child, Linda was Grandmother Nannie's favorite.

I, like my Mother and Grandmother Susie, am dark-skinned with teeth that protruded with spaces. I sucked all four of my fingers in my mouth at one time. I was skinny; my hair wasn't long and fine. My hair would curl like lambs wool. Linda called me Black Samba. One would never have known that Linda and I had different Fathers. One day a letter came with my first name Tasha and a different last name. It said to call Aunt Jean. Well, Mother told me and I told Linda the story. You're not my "Whole Sister". Anyway, Linda told me to move out because this was her Daddy's house.

Linda called me a "Step Child". The next thing I knew was that we were fighting. We began fighting so badly until one of the next door neighbors called to our parents. Daddy came outdoors with the belt and whipped us both. Debra our youngest sister merely looked at us get our whipping from Daddy. Did this black belt hurt? It was about 32" long and 1" thick with a silver buckle on it. I got the whipping first for being the oldest and then for fighting outdoors. I always was the fighter. I had to protect Linda because she wouldn't ever fight. Daddy told us that he'd better not hear of us embarrassing him anymore, after all he loved us both the same. He warned us about being like "Tomboys". He told us he had better not hear the term "half-sister" or "step child" anymore coming from our mouths.

In those days one's skin color was very important. Since being Dark like me was a shame I naturally picked Girlfriends that were Light Skinned. The Light Skinned girls with curly hair got invited out on all the dates, she got invited to the real nice parties. Only then did the guys notice you because you were with the light skinned girl. This hurt badly. Why did I have to be born this color? Why is my hair so nappy, Mother? Why didn't you pick a man with nice features? You see my sister would feel that she was better than me. Her skin was lighter than mine. She felt that she could take my boyfriend because her color was lighter than mine. Our voices were so similar. The phone would ring and she'd talk to my boyfriend. "Hi, this is me. Yeah, come on over. I'll be ready at Eight O'clock PM." The phone would start clicking because the third party (three party phone) would want to use the telephone. Actually the third party would start talking on the phone. I'd have to hang up the phone. To my sister, this was funny.

Those White Castles were the best cheeseburgers. They were juicy and smelled so good. They were thicker then. The waitress' uniforms were black and white checked. They wore little aprons and a white headband with the White Castle emblem. One's tray was often knocked off the car because of one smooch (hugging and kissing) or whatever in the car. While eating our Cheeseburgers, the R adio would be playing the song "Oh, What a Night" by the Dells. This song made one want to forever stay on the Ole Miss. The Old Mississippi River if it could talk, it would tell many a story. Huckleberry Finn wrote many tales about this famous river that runs through several Southern states. It now has the famous monument called the Gateway to the West that stands on the St. Louis, Missouri 's Riverbank.

Our favorite pizza was sausage and cheese. I couldn't eat sausage at home because the religion called eating pork a sin. Was this good stuff! The cheese would come off in strands all over our shorts. My date and my friend's date belonged to the motorcycle gang. Of course we wouldn't ride the motorcycles to the drive-in. Actually, their first child was a boy. He was so cute. His hair was blonde and curly. They soon moved to Los Angeles and left me in St. Louis. Here I was going to school by bus everyday to a neighborhood where my Mother wanted me to go and my newest best friend was leaving me in St. Louis. I began to dislike this mess. All of the students in the Nineth grade were in what we called "Little Sumner". "Little Sumner High School Annex" was set aside in a different building to assimilate all of the freshman to central records due to the integration of all the public schools in the city of St. Louis which began in 1954. Segerated Education was illegal – no more Separate (Segration of students)

I had to go to a school that I didn't want to go to. Mother got a special permit for me to go to this high school that was out of the district that I lived in. She wanted me to attend the "best high school". I made up my mind that I would excel.

I joined the Student Council, the Girls Glee Club, wrote a column in the School Newspaper and wrote Poetry for the Yearbook. I wanted to be a Cheerleader but I wasn't limber enough, or was it because of my brown skin? The football game in St. Louis was traditionally between two schools - Sumner High School Bulldogs and the Vashon High School Wolverines. The Maroon and White versus the Blue and White. Old Public School Stadium was located in the "West End."

Vashon almost always won each "Turkey Day Game". They were tougher and if you dated a guy on Vashon's football team the two schools formed a gang to settle who the girl would date. Fights were fist fights only, the band would look out their windows from the bus and laugh.

My poetry for the high school yearbook, wouldn't you know, was all an expression of my love to my son's father. I was so in love. The inevitable had to happen. I became pregnant in my senior year of high school. Well, I told the father that I was pregnant. He told me that he was joining the Foreign Legion. He didn't join the Legion; instead he joined the United States Navy. I didn't know how to find him. Finally, my son was born and, of course, I heard from his father then. My son weighed 9 pounds, 4 ounces.

I've always been a romantic. "Darling You Send Me" was a popular song recorded by Sam Cooke. This guy knew I was a romantic. Although we were young, we felt that we were in love. While visiting his mother and father with our newborn son, we became closer. We then decided we would marry and raise our son together as man and wife. After all, we sent each other to the tune of Sam Cooke's melody.

My father-in-law was a Baptist Minister. My mother-in-law was totally against the marriage. She threatened to hurt me if I married her son. She verbalized those threats. However, as long as her son and I didn't marry, she was happy. She accepted her grandson readily. The truth of her resentment was that she was a mother at Fifteen Years Old. She could not finish high school because she had to care for her child, my Son's father. She never let her son's father know that he had been born.

She was never able to be happy with being a Maid. She resented the fact that I was a High School Graduate, working as a Secretary and about to marry her Son.

I was not the only unmarried "mother-to-be" in the senior class. There were three others. One is a very successful World Known Singer. . She told us she would be Rich and Famous one day.

Since we couldn't march down the aisle on Graduation Night, our Principal delivered our diplomas to each home the next day. I can never forget how hurt my Mother and Father were. My Mother hid my pregnancy from my Father by sending me off each morning to my Grandmother's house.

Dad and the neighbors assumed that I was going to school every day. The "Chemis Dress" was very popular then in 1957, 1958. Of course, today the style is popular again some twenty-four or twenty-five years later. Oh, this means I'm seeing the style come back again. Time waits for no one. One thing was certain I could feel proud of myself.

I had graduated from high school; had a beautiful healthy baby and had a good job. I worked for a well established organization. I just needed more money in order to give my Son more. The salary I earned was not enough. I had to pay the babysitter and travel to and from work. The Allotment from my Husband's Navy salary was placed in an account to set us up in our home once he was discharged. We never saw the home. The money was spent to buy his Grey and White 'Nineteen Fifty-Five used Buick. It didn't take long for me to see that Marriage to him would be short-lived. His income from his job as a Fireman was spent on his fun. He forgot about his responsibilities to his Son and me. He would not buy Groceries or pay the Rent; let alone depositing money in the Savings Account. All of our bills went unpaid. Then he left and moved to Los Angeles, California. He became involved in selling drugs in L.A. and eventually went to jail. His mother had to constantly go through her savings, or borrow money to pay her son's Legal fees. It became a family affair of raising money to keep him out of jail. It became a family affair with being a pimp.

After our divorce, he married a School Teacher who he beat with hangers across her face, legs and back if she didn't obey this man. I never was exposed to this physical abuse by this guy, my son's father. Was I glad I had been spared this kind of abuse! I was far removed from his insane behavior. I needed another job to defray all of these expenses alone. I hired a lawyer to Sue my Son's Father for Non-Support. This was very hard, but it was done. He would hide from Constable or Sheriff after his Mother informed him that I was beginning to collect Child Support Payments. She was outraged and told me she never asked her Son's Father for a Dime in support of him. After all, she could not. Maybe he would never have believed her claim of Paternity anyway. No wonder in reflecting back I can see why she resented me so strongly.

As life moves on, I did find a good friend amidst all of those professionals at Homer G. Phillips and the jet setters on the St. Louis up and coming scene. He, of course, is still my friend. I'd have to say that if anyone was a model for my behavior and discipline regarding completion of my educational goals he was the one. His family was one group of people who maintained strong ties. They were very proud to be members of their community, "The Ville". This young man worked at the United States Post Office and the Department of Housing and Urban Development. He attended school for 10 years at night simultaneously and maintained his family and home all at the same time. Today, he has resigned working for the government and has his own property consultant firm. I'd say we encouraged each other. It was with his help, care and concern that enabled me to make the transition from St. Louis to New Jersey move so swiftly. This individual has so much good influence on me. I began to copy his lifestyle. I resigned from Homer G. Phillips Hospital only to work for the Jefferson-Cass Health Center. Here I would not be losing my City Civil Service Employee Status but I was able to work a straight shift. I could finally attend school at night like my friend.

My Son had grown large enough for me to be away from him. I knew that I had to acquire another skill to earn a decent income. I saw various professionals working here at the Health Center. I then made up my mind which curriculum I would pursue to earn a college degree. This was hard. I needed a good Babysitter. This was "double trouble". I reflected on what had happened to me. I prayed that I'd get the right person to care for my Son. The problem quickly resolved itself. I am grateful for those people who assisted in providing child care.

I enrolled at Forest Park Community College to work toward an Associate in Liberal Arts Degree. I attended school at night for seven years. I could not keep this pace going any longer. I had to make a decision to become a full time student or forever work and go to school. Amidst all of these problems my grades remained good. They were so good that I was accepted at the St. Louis University Undergraduate School of Social Service. Mother and Dad and

Byron attended the graduation ceremony at Forest Park Community College. I was happy to be accepted at St. Louis University.

I had no idea of how I would be able to afford to go to a Jesuit Institution. I prayed; I asked God to allow me to get through the door. I'd be given a way by God's help to get through St. Louis University. The Lord answered my prayers. My blessings were so well received from God that I received both a Bachelors of Social Work and a Masters of Social Work degree from that institution. Mother, Daddy and my youngest Sister attended my undergraduate graduation ceremony. My Son helped me put on my Cap and Gown.

Through the friend whom I met at the hospital, I then graciously and expeditiously moved through selling the property in St. Louise with another highly successful realty firm. A lot of problems existed in selling property that I was unaware of. All I knew was that I could no longer pay rent in New Jersey and make mortgage payments. My salary would not permit it. Through Divorce Court Settlement I was the sole owner of the property in University City. I was now able to sell the property and the proceeds of the sale came to me. We're talking about some $50,000 sale. My ex-husband had taken out a $16,000 Small Business Administration (SBA) loan to purchase a deficient business. A music' store was going out of business. I attempted to explain to my husband that the neighborhoods that once thrived in St. Louis after World War II and the Korean War were rapidly decaying after the riots of the 60's. People that lived in the inner city were moving to the suburbs. The '78 RPM (Rounds/Record) were going out of existence. The new 45 RPM's were taking their place. The old juke boxes or stereos were seeing a more expensive, highly sophisticated component set gradually take its place. Obviously, more capital had to be available, more larger national music firms were pushing the smaller individual owners nationwide out of business. Of course, he resented my valuable insight. The owner had more influence than I. He had worked for the owner since he was 15 years old. He had dropped out of high school in the 9th grade to help take care of his single mother and his 9 brothers and sisters. Her existence was derived from Welfare Aid to Dependent Children from East St. Louis, Illinois. The owner had assisted, of course, in caring for the entire family in time of crisis. You know this guy fell for this "False Dream of Owning His Own Business" to the point of telling me that he had to use our $25,000 home as collateral in addition to the SBA $16,000 loan. This owner had four music shops. He sold each store for $16,000. Each new owner had to buy all of the fixtures, purchase his music supply accounts and pay his bills. My husband almost threatened to kill me if I didn't go along with his newly acquired business. The previous owner received a check from the Small Business Administration and went into a "Quick Photostatic" copying firm in new corporate structures. All but one of the businesses died. My husband had never seen that kind of money in his life. He thought it lasted forever. His employees had no knowledge of how to run or manage a business. They were allowed access to the small amount of income that derived from the business. After 6 months, they immediately left town with money they stole from my ex-husband's bank account and cash register. One day, I got a notice in the mail of default on SBA repayment. Then I told my husband that he would have to close the business. Everything would be auctioned off. I didn't act alarmed. It was amazing that it lasted two years. Shortly thereafter, I noticed he began to stay out on weekends. My son was at least Fourteen Years Old. The influence that he had on my son began to scare me. Although I was still attending school and working full time, I did see the handwriting on the wall. It spelled "doom". I could not believe that this guy rejected everything that I said regarding his life, mine and my son's future. Well, I did see its ugly head. He refused to do any type of gainful work. He refused to repay the debt, he returned to live in a shack that had holes in the floor. His whole attitude was awful. His appearance was downtrodden. He had lost his identity.

I was pressed for time to report to work in New Jersey and all of these things to stop me from reporting. A dear friend and neighbor, who now lives in Hawaii, drove with me and helped me resettle in New Jersey. We cried when we departed. I paid his plane fare back to St. Louis out of the small amount of money received from the sale of the house. The realtor became a friend indeed. He did not charge the usual sales commission because the Small Business Administration would not allow me too much profit. No, I don't care to tell you the amount I received from the sale. The realtor felt sorry for the way things turned out. He is not only selling real estate today he is doing land development and owns franchises with a very profitable fast food chain out of Atlanta, Georgia. Speaking of a blessing and miracles being performed, what else could I attribute these events to?

Of course, today tales/rumors exist that I had affairs with all of my male friends. I have more male friends than I do female friends anyway. It's not because I seduce them. It's because I'm no threat to them, their families or their being. They are secure individuals. Secure individuals be they male or female are very comfortable around me. After all which do we tend to help more - a child or an adult if they are strangers within our midst? I'd dare say that we would offer assistance to the child before we offer help to a stranger that's an adult. Why? Because we fear that the adult would harm us.

Chapter III

SEXISM

I can remember the first supervisor who would call me into his office and rub his genitals in front of me after it became erected. He would laugh and tell me I was Miss "P.T." ("P.T." stood for "Prick Teaser") I didn't like that at all. He called me last Christmas long distance to tell me that I would never be able to live in St. Louis because all of the men remember me as "Miss Sexy". He went so far as to say that I screwed all of the men in St. Louis. He said, "You know I'll be coming to New Jersey this summer and I'd like to see you." I'm afraid if he sees me he'll carry out all of his fantasies. He is now divorced from his wife who probably found out about all of his attempted and actual sexual encounters (extra-marital) flings. Well, he had a grape vine. He told policemen, doctors, lawyers, fraternal organizations of his staff member. I worked a rotating shift that meant I was on duty on the midnight shift. The Emergency Room kept me in contact with a lot of men in all walks of life. "Tails Tell Tales". I realized what my supervisor had done so I had to handle it. It became an "inferiority complex".

Doctors and nurses found this to be good news. I was so sexy until I was invited to the "Wild Parties". One night, a Doctor was caught having Sexual Intercourse on an operating room table with a nurse. Do you know they called me to come to the operating room to take a report? A patient had died in surgery from a gun shot wound to the stomach. I told them I could not leave my area. Lo and behold, the police came to the area to type their report. Was I sickened to think that they wanted to include me in such acts?

One Halloween, I can remember that a very close friend of mine from elementary school was having a fling with a young single doctor. She was married to a policeman and had four small children. She worked as a switchboard operator. She told her co-worker. The switchboard operator knew of the couple's rendezvous. She telephoned the husband and told him the tale of where the couple could be found. They both died in each other's arms while making love - victims of the policeman's bullet. The doctor's casket was never opened. His family came and took his body back to his place of birth for burial. Everyone from the hospital, or so it appeared, came to the switchboard operator's funeral. The husband served only three years in jail. Today he is a successful businessman.

Every Christmas, everyone mourned the couple's death. People returned home for the holidays. Party, party, party. As a matter of fact we had a "Round Robin".

A Round Robin party was parties given simultaneously at different individual's houses. Entertainment consisted of catered food of various types, liquor galore and any other medium to get high. This could be sex, movies, or drugs. After all, this was the jet-set, the in-crowd, the up and coming black urban professionals. Men nor women would wear the same thing twice. Who was the first one to buy their home in the suburbs? Who was the first one to open his office? How good was his practice? Can he or she survive after Med or Law school? Who is that who got their Mercedes, Porsche or Peugeot? Who has the biggest diamond cocktail ring? Hey, who's telling the tale and do you have it right according to the grapevine? Did you get invited to the Frat House Party at the Kappa or the Q's house on Westminster? Did you hear about Dr. Love's party at the Vagabonds on Westminster Place? The bar on Taylor and Finney Avenue had been the in-place bar for the West End crowd. To further say you're still in the "In-Crowd" after you die depended upon what funeral home handled the final rites. They even looked for the bronze coffin as a symbol of status. If the coffin was bronze and glass enclosed, it rarely meant "upper class". My first job allowed me access into the In-crowd. This would make me or break me. "The Four Just Men" came about. These were a group of postal employees that formed a social organization to raise money to continue to have formal affairs for those who were not affiliated with a fraternity or sorority.

"I'm in with the in-crowd, I go where the in-crowd goes". That was the tune recorded by Ramsey Lewis and his trio. Ramsey Lewis' tune was a number one seller that year. Boy was I having fun. I made it my business to purchase the most sexually attractive party wear. I wore dresses that were low cut in the back and V-shaped or halter top. One was made out of green organza with a fitted top, sleeveless and a group of four wide ruffles that were white at the bottom. My stockings had a back seam with rhinestones on the side. My favorite outfit was a yellow jumpsuit with splits in the legs on the outside. The splits began at the upper thigh. Of course the front was low cut. Then I learned to be "T Totally" sexy. You wear perfume that isn't Avon. You buy Estee Lauder Youth Dew Perfume and perfumed bath oil. You place it on the pulse points of the body. That is at the back of both knees where the legs bend. When wearing panty hose the fragrance gets all in your clothing. You also place a drop of perfume behind the ear lobes; you place a drop on the inside of both wrists. You place body smooth silk lotion 49 allover the body. That fragrance will emanate from you all night long. Don't worry that you will dance so hard that all of your fragrance will be gone. It'll only come off when you take a bath or shower.

Make-up is essential. It enhances what you already have. Make-up consisted of foundation cream, eye shadow, eye liner, mascara and pencil to match the color of the outfit that I would wear. Contour powder was needed to highlight the cheekbones, demi-stick was used to cover any lines or blemishes in the face. Demi-stick was used to cover pimples or make the nose appear smaller. It can also make the lips take on either a smaller or bigger appearance as needed. I went to many a make-up artist class to learn the techniques.

You aren't the only one smelling like Estee Lauder, or Norrell, or Shalimar, or Charlie. The men were into wearing their fragrances. Men wore Canoe, Aramus, or Karl Lagerfields. Um, that scent is so sexy. It's actually fun to have the senses aroused to this point. Of course, some of the guys had the tendency to overdo the fragrance but hey—it's all in fun. After all we are going to party and party hardy all night long. Everyone was everyone in order to get on the party invitation list. Brothers from Tennessee State, Howard U. and Lincoln University were all there. Omegas, Alphas, Deltas, Sigmas AKAs, we all partied. The Isley's "It's Your Thing, Do What You Wanna Do" rang from the various houses that participated in the Round Robin.

The menus consisted of collard greens with ham hocks, corn bread, fried chicken, chitterlings, hog malls, ham, turkey, macaroni and cheese, potato salad, lettuce and tomatoes, radishes and cucumbers arranged pretty on a tray. Liquor consisted of Dry Sack, Tanqueray Gin, Harvey's Bristol Cream Cherry Wine, Johnnie Walker Red Scotch and beer. Mixers were Seven-Up, Ginger-Ale, Seltzer Water and Roses Lime Juice. Drinks were garnished with lime or lemon twist.

The fun was in the air. Cars of people would arrive. They'd give the "code word" to get in. Some would bring liquor with them and some wouldn't. It didn't matter, next month they'd host a party.

The dance was the Bump, the record was "Fire" by the Ohio Players. The Bump could be considered a sensuous dance. The guys could really maneuver their curves to fit into my curves. The lights were turned down low. Red lights, blue lights and disco lights flashed on and off to the sound of the bass tones from the stereo speakers. The Penquin, the Monkey, the Dog, the Stroll and the Bop were the dances that were popular during that era. Johnny Taylor's "Who's Making Love To Your Old Lady" seemed to set the tone of the party around 3:00 AM. Everyone was really feeling good by this time. The effects of the liquor combined with the Herb (marijuana) and Cocaine, or uppers, or bennies was causing all sorts of things to happen. In these days, it was "safe" to do "Mary Jane" or "Do-Bee". Do your thing, baby. This was

during the Viet Nam era. Everyone was into peace and loving. It was ok for parents to allow their kids to smoke marijuana. In fact, the parents and kids could smoke marijuana together. Parties sometimes allowed the kids and three or four of their friends to assist in serving refreshments.

It was 1968. The Ten Year First High School Reunion of the '58 Class of Sumner High School came about. We enjoyed seeing each other, and seeing who had moved from one plateau to another. Of course my son was now 10 years old. He was glad that we had moved from inner city to suburbs.

One thing was for sure. I wasn't ashamed of my handsome son, I had just moved into my own house, I had a new '68 convertible beige Oldsmobile. I strictly left behind all of the religious upbringing that I knew. My husband hadn't attended church either. The one goal of going to my class reunion as Mrs. was accomplished. I had nothing to be ashamed of. As a matter of fact one of the class reunion meetings was held at my house. We held the meeting at various class members' homes to discuss plans for the gala activity. Many of my fellow classmates were very successful. We had fields ranging from accounting to nursing to education, to singing and of course housewives. Our teacher who spoke at the occasion told us we still looked like we were walking the halls of Sumner. We all wished that it was true; although it sounded good.

Adulthood also saw me getting depressed and upset with the way things were going. I made up my mind that I'd take matters in my hands. College education would place me above being sexually harassed. My body is causing me to experience all of this pain. I wish I was a boy. Boys don't have to put up with having them played with. All boys and men do is make my life miserable. I then started reading the Kinsey Report and Masters' and Johnsons' books in attempts to try to know what was going on. I especially knew nothing of what I was doing. I kept reading the word orgasm. I wanted to know what an orgasm was. I then read about oral sex. I wanted to know what that was. I read about lesbians. This really sounded weird. My Mother then told me how dangerous all of these books were. I would attempt to hide them under my bedsprings but she found them. I then wanted to know about all of these things. I even read about bestiality. What's that? I read in Revelations in the Bible about the beast in the last days of the earth's existence. How does this all connect, I wondered? Finally, my girlfriend and I got together with these books down at her house at night. We'd go to her Aunt and ask her questions. Her name was Jane. She was always open and honest. She had a cousin who was in the U.S. Army. He was being discharged. He was attracted to me. He was such a gentleman. He came to my parent's home and asked to take me out on a date. He was very dark. He didn't look like most of my boyfriends that I dated. He dressed extremely well. He would wear creases down the center of jeans no less. He'd have his shoes shined even though he wore jeans. I liked him very much. He always carried prophylactics in his pocket. He would always sneak his penis in me because he had been overseas in the Korean War. He knew how to have sex and not be noticed while doing it. It was fun with him. He knew how to hold me when we would go to the rooming house. He knew more places to go that were rented out for a few hours. You'd be in the process of a real steamy love making session and someone would knock on the door and yell "time's up". This was a big business on Friday and Saturday night. Often right after going to a movie, this is the way your date ended. These were houses that looked like an ordinary family dwelling. Once inside, you'd see the desk with a book on it. Then a man or lady would stand there and say, "How long will you be?" The guy would answer. Of course, I wasn't asked how long I'd like to stay. All of these moments are reflected upon as one has become of age. Why is sex so important? It seems as if the world evolves around SEX.

"Mister, get your hands off of my buttocks. It belongs to my body not your hands. Rubbing your body up against mine in the elevator, or on the bus makes me angry. Your suggestions as to whether or not we are going to have sex before you can take me out on a date tonight only makes me say I don't want to go out with you. I don't want to have to repay you with my body." Sex is beautiful though.

Adulthood was a combination of motherhood, divorce and career. Somehow, I thought that getting a professional education would cause one not to experience sexual harassment or advancements. I felt that one's education would do. I would be respected for me and not my body. That was not the case. Supervisors and/or bosses desired me to go to bed to keep the job or to get a promotion. I never have gotten to management or supervisory status because my basic premise is that one's body or sexuality has nothing to do with one's ability to do a job.

You know after a while one has to accept himself. How is this possible when from the time of being four years old, you can remember your relatives fondling your body, playing with your erotic zones.

Your uncle or your cousin laying on the floor on a blanket reading you nursery rhymes. All of a sudden you feel a hard penis against your buttocks. It never penetrated. It was just rubbed against my leg. Oh, I was scared. This thing looked so horrible. It was big and hard. He kept saying it won't hurt. Don't cry. I am going to show you where it goes. You can't tell anyone about our afternoon naps together. I can remember the wetness and him breathing hard while laying next to me. I kept saying Uncle what's wrong. He just kept wriggling his body in sexual gyrations until he would reach an orgasm with his finger, massaging my vagina.

The baby sitter was my mother's friend. Do you know my parents still do not know about those times to this day? This lady and her sister kept me and two other children. They would have me cuddled in one of their laps and would make me suck their nipples. Then

I would have to place my hand on the other breast. This one in particular didn't wear underpanties. She would take my hand and place it wherever she wanted me to place it. I could remember feeling something soft and hairy and wet. When I tried to remove my hand, she would pull it hard and hold it in place. This smelled awful. My hand was wet and I would run to the bathroom and wash my hands. I told her I was going to tell my mother. She whipped me and said you'll get beaten if you tell her. Tomorrow, you'll feel better after your mother goes to work. Her sister (the baby sitter) wasn't any better. She would play with the little boy's genitals. She'd massage his penis and kiss his body. She, also, made him suck her breast. We would have to watch. We were scared to tell our parents. These women were seeking sexual satisfaction through us. The thing that hurt worst was when they would make the little boys put themselves inside of us. They made the two of us stand against the wall, remove our clothes and touch, caress and kiss each other's bodies. If the little boys did not know where to touch the little girls or the little girls did not know where to touch the little boys, they assisted in placing everything where it belonged. This never left my mind. It will never leave. It will always make me question the validity of any type of intimate relationship. It had a damaging effect for life. But I've made it. There is hope.

The only thing bad about going through these bad experiences so early in life is that it makes you interact as a sexual thing only. No one can want me for me. They want your body in a position in bed. I'm more than a vagina. I actually had guys say to me you looked like you wanted me to ask you to take you to bed. Your body drips in sex. But I try to wear clothes that cover me up. Oh, is that funny to them. As a little girl I felt that I was ugly. Short hair, black skin, teeth that stuck out and had spaces. I'm just made to be pawned.

Fifteen years of marriage that was lived in nightmarish fashion took it's toll on me and my son. It was at the point of all the purity being gone. He didn't want me. He wanted my body. I'm not a sex machine. Sex is spontaneous and beautiful. It's an interaction between two people that love each other. We took vows. For good or bad we were to be together 'til death.

I thought about mother and dad's marriage. Their marriage seemed to be solid, pure and good. Mother and dad have celebrated not 15, but 35 years of marriage. How and what is the secret ingredient in a marriage that keeps a couple together? Do those women have to tolerate what I wouldn't bear? You see one thing for certain, there was no free communication between my mother and myself on this level of intimacy. My son and I would discuss freely his relationships as opposed to the discussion that mother and I would have. You see I'll never know what she withstood in order to celebrate that many years of "togetherness".

Not only do I wonder about mother and dad's relationship, but I think of others that I've had many contacts with. Often many clients would say to me, "Oh, you're Miss? You'd better be glad." I'd attempt to find out the reasons for their statements and I would be told some of the unhappiness, some of the many intolerable or unbearable incidents that these women are living with. They look to me and say you've made it and can be independent. You don't have to wash anyone's clothes but your own. You don't have to put up with feeling like an object instead of a human being. Well listen, I wouldn't go through it again for all the wealth in the world. Back to my scenes.

The underwear was repulsive, the type that you'd buy in Frederick's of Hollywood or Adam's Apple, but I was to join in on the "Swinger's Sex Parties". This meant having other couples over to our house for food, sex and booze. This meant sharing the most intimate act that a married couple could enjoy. Where was the love? What about our child? What if the child would get up out of bed and wander from his bedroom to ours by mistake? He would see all of these naked people, hear all of these strange sounds, smell the stench of booze, marijuana and sex. My God, what had I gotten into? I was then ready to end everything.

I discussed my bewildered marriage with one of my college advisors. He told me that I should feel honored to have men view me as such. Not only did the opposite sex see me as a sex object but I was getting the same reaction or interaction from the same sex at this time in my life.

I remember distinctly my grade school teacher in Encounter #1. This lady was single. She had never married. She was very tall, she had dimples. She was very well liked by all the parents. No one had any idea that I had experienced these encounters with her, I'm sure. Maybe others in the class had similar experiences and were also afraid to tell.

Once the shades were lowered and the doors locked, no one was in the building except the janitor. She would take me to a stall in the girl's bathroom and began her most bewildering acts. No wonder children grow up being self-conscious about their sexuality. You can't imagine what these sick adults do to young, vulnerable children. I was the "Teacher's Pet". I would bite her nipple when she'd mash my head against her breast. Then she'd hold me like the babysitter did on her lap. She'd scare me by saying if I didn't suck her the nice way she'd leave me in the toilet, lock the door and let the rats and mice eat me up. Do you know one time she locked the bathroom door? I screamed and hollered, but it did no good. I had been a bad girl.

I can remember my buttocks being rubbed by a hand through the space in back of the seat part of the desk from the boy behind me. Or maybe the boy in the desk in front of me sticking his hand between the seat back feeling my leg. Again little boys would do what their babysitters had taught them to do to the little girls. This would make me angry and I'd hit him or tell the teacher by raising my hand interrupting her presentation. You're a troublemaker! You're making the little boys do that to you. You make people feel you. You make people call you names. You're a troublemaker. You start fights. Yes, I would protect myself from being fondled by teachers, students or whoever.

My husband had the audacity to ask me to have a child for him. I
had a fit. I didn't want anymore children. I attempted to carry for at
least three months, but I kept noticing that my panties were spotting
blood. Finally I saved some money to have an abortion. In those days,
abortions only cost $105.00. I was so scared, but I knew I had to do
it. The doctor asked me why I wanted to do it. You could take a coat
hanger and jab it up your vagina. You'd start bleeding and go to the
hospital and they'd put you on the operating room table and you'd
get a D & C. Boom, the baby was gone. My husband never knew the
truth. This doctor had given so many abortions to so many of my
girlfriends. Abortions were illegal then. There was a code word you
use before you'd be approved by the doctor. My grandmother was a
maid for the doctor which helped me to get through the maze. One
of my girlfriends took a set of knitting needles and bled to death.
She didn't make it. I prayed that I'd be here to see my son become
an adult. I managed to walk down the steps from the doctor's office
alone and get home and lay in the bed. By then, I was having severe
cramps. It was hurting so bad. My grandmother assisted me. She came
to my house and had the water pail ready. All of a sudden with the
rubber sheet under me I yelled and here was a fetus. A white small
object that looked like a tiny doll with no color or pigmentation to
it. I became scared then. I realized that I had taken a life. I prayed
to God for forgiveness. I could never ever let my son know. It looked
like a female embryo. The tiny fingers, the tiny toes, the eyelids; that
was it. My menses lasted several weeks. I finally went back for my six
week examination. By then, I was thoroughly upset with my life.

There was this very dear friend who had been my boyfriend all
along. He was crying throughout the ordeal. Everyone knew about us
except my husband. In his circle of friends, I was known as his next
wife. I feel to this day that he loved me. We attended many house
parties in the same "Round Robin" sequel. Again, color became an
issue. He was light, fair-skinned with curly hair. His wife was of the
same "blue-veined" complexion. That is light skinned black folk.

They were from the other side of town. At least I know he did love me. Some of our episodes were truly dangerous. Every day, we would see each other at work. I'd go meet him for lunch. I'd go by his house, he'd come by my house. Well, he finally started dating one of my dark-skinned girlfriends. I started dating one of his light-skinned friends who was more successful in his career than he was.

The inevitable of my having to have a clean sweep (hysterectomy) came about. I became scared. Once a woman has a hysterectomy she loses all of her sex appeal. My doctor a very prominent OB-GYN Jewish practitioner assured me that I'd have a "cradle minus the baby". I said what does that mean? He was so handsome and yet so kind, and so smart. He assured me that sex would be better. He told me my vagina would become smaller because he was sewing it up at the area where it usually stretched.

I couldn't think about sex anymore. All I knew was that I had endometriosis. I had many, many tumors on the lining of my womb that had to be removed. I had severe pain upon menstruation. Instead of the blood being bright red it was dark almost black in color. It had a foul odor. Oh, I'm going to die. I'm going to die with cancer. I'd seen several of my close friends die with that stuff. I'll kill myself before I die like that. Those people die with a terrible odor. The smell never leaves your senses. My doctor then had to work on alleviating me of the fear. Finally the day for the surgery arrived. He scheduled it for a winter day. That way the bleeding wouldn't be so profuse. Mother came to stay with me to assist me in walking to and from the bed; and to help with my son and caring for him.

Surprising, my husband was very kind. He brought me a great big black and white teddy bear that must have been at least 4 feet tall. He had a bright red ribbon on his neck. I hugged him while I lay in bed with that giant sanitary pad on. I had to wear the sanitary belt that you'd wear after having a baby. I still worried about taking on male features. My doctor told me that he'd save the ovaries. Therefore, I'd have my secondary female characteristics. The day came for me as per my doctor's instructions to start taking Betadine douches and bathes. Oh, no!!! You mean for me to touch myself. You mean for me to put a douche stem inside of my vagina. As it is when I wipe myself, I'm getting black or grey matter on the toilet paper or my sanitary pad. Now you're saying take douches two times per day. "Yes, two times each day or you can cause more problems that will come about as a result of you not taking the douches."

My lover of "x amount of years" became scared for sure then. All of a sudden I wasn't sexually appealing to him. I was already scared of myself. I was dry because I wasn't stimulated by him. All he wanted to do was to see if I was able to do what we used to do. How could I? He didn't kiss, hug, pet, rub my breast or play with my nipples as we use to do. He didn't play with my clitoris or anything he used to do. The only thing he wanted to do was to penetrate. It didn't work because I wasn't pre-sexually stimulated. Well, he really let me know that he needed a partner that sexually motivated him. He then let me know in no specific nice words that he was dating my girlfriend or my supposed to be girlfriend. Was I hurt!! My husband almost caught us at a large social function on the dance floor dancing as if we were married. Anyway I did regroup. I attended lectures about how to cope after having a hysterectomy. I learned that pre-sexual (foreplay) was very important. Sex would not be gratifying without it. As a matter of fact some women had to use a vaginal lubricant. One thing, I did begin to enjoy sex again. I was in a double-bind situation. I wanted to be sexually attractive, but only when I wanted to. My husband went out of his way to make me look sexy. It went from me feeling good about being sexy to myself and to him also. But he went overboard.

0Once he became aware of my non-enjoyment of his pleasure, he became closer to my son. He tried to keep up with him. He'd call him to come to his job. He'd give him his car and try to talk against me to my son. It was obvious to him that our marriage was ending.

My son had become confused. He looked at me strange and began to experiment with sex, alcohol and drugs.

High school teachers felt that they could really do what they wanted to and never worry about anyone telling of their activity with you. Their approach was entirely different. The teacher would come to my house and help me with Mathematics; my worse course. Well he'd talk to Mother and tell her we were going to the Library. The Library was the back seat of the car. My legs spread open, his finger inserted in my vagina before the penis was inserted. He didn't insist on two episodes. He didn't want to arouse Mother's suspicion. We then would go to the Public Library and I'd be drilled on how to do a problem. He always gave me special attention. I actually liked him very much. He was married and had two daughters. One has to question his rationale for such acts. He was so nice, he looked good. My grade in Math was B. I knew I wasn't able to do Algebra or Geometry. Anyway he never stopped being my friend. Well I had another high school teacher/pupil encounter. This teacher was all together different.

I excelled in business courses, I then wanted to become an executive secretary. I was good in shorthand, typing and spelling. I spoke English well. I wrote well. I was going to work for McDonnell Douglass Aircraft Corp. I said. Well this teacher knew how to trap me. He told me that he knew most of the big executives and he'd get me a job. However, he'd call me after dinner time and tell me he was coming to take me to the executive officer who was waiting for me. He was offering his time, I said he's kind. I asked him how could I pay him when I had no money. He smiled. We would never come inside the house and talk to my parents like my Math teacher did. His main objective wasn't obvious because he had distinguished it by waiting outside in the car at a certain designated time. According to him, we were rushing to the executive's office.

After finally riding around McDonnell's office complex and his hand moving over touching my legs in a very firm grip, I knew he was lying about his intentions. I said, "Why did you lie? You want me to go to the back seat don't you?" He said no. "We don't have to go to the back seat. Just sit on my lap and I can put it in. You have on a wide skirt. No one will know what we're doing." He was very persistent. I tried to move away and he scratched my leg. He attempted to tear up my underwear and throw it away. Here it was the winter time. He could only keep the motor running so long in the car because it was cold. When the motor was turned off, the steam would turn to frost. I knew I couldn't fight and win, so I just let him do what he enjoyed doing. I certainly didn't enjoy myself. All of that cold weather to add insult to injury and me with nothing but my coat and socks on. He kept his coat and all of his clothes on though. Do women have it rough?

The church wasn't a big help because boys would do the same thing at church as they did at school. One of the church ministers also had fondled me many, many times. He wasn't married either. He led me to believe that he'd marry me. At least I wasn't coerced into having sexual intercourse.

The high school teachers would spread rumors about me to my male classmates. If they could have sexual favors, then I'd get an "A". At this point, I felt there was no use. Maybe it was true, I was created just for people to act out their sexual desires. At that time, I took a real hard look at myself. I then began to hate the way that I looked. School, church, neighbors, babysitters, why did I have to be born I asked many times. No, I never thought about ending my life as a teenager, but I sure wanted answers. Even though we had to go to church because of parental demands, it wasn't the answer either.

These are tales of my younger years. Next, you'll read what activity the tails perform. They use their paws to pawn over me. It's a wonder that I didn't commit suicide. Young people weren't committing suicide as much back then. In my mind, anyway, as Daddy said, "Suicide was an unforgiveable sin". You can't take away your life. Only God giveth and God taketh away. No one understands me.

Chapter IV

PAWNING, PAWS

We lived in a six family adjoining row house in the rear of the business district located in midtown St. Louis. We lived at 3234 (rear) Olive Street on the second floor. I both lived in and went to the schools in the same area. Both my lowest and highest level of education came from the same area. St. Louis University School of Social Service was located exactly three blocks from our house. The school is located on Lindell Boulevard, we stayed on Olive Street. Actually, Olive Street and Lindell Boulevard come together at one intersection, Compton Street and then separate and run parallel along their paths to the more rich areas in St. Louis suburbia.

I can also visualize living there from the time of my being three years old. The place was so small. Here it was a two room, second floor row flat that had to be entered through a gangway. My best Christmas was also had in this two room house. Daddy sure enjoyed his three little girls. We'd wait for him to pick us up. By him being 6'3" tall it felt like we were on top of a roof. Besides, he'd pick us up after climbing thirty stairs. We'd play on the porch with our toys, our coloring books, and jacks and ball. We had a bolo bat. It was a wooden paddle with a handle on it that had a ball attached to a long strand of rubber. The one who paddled the most without missing the ball's continuous beat was the winner. My skills in these areas were needing a lot to be desired.

Boys would play with their marbles. They'd always like playing with our bolo bat. They also had yo-yos. They'd flip their wrist and the object would fallout fast and return with one flip of the wrist. The boys also played a game called Hambone. This was done by hitting or slapping their opened hand against their upper thigh to the beat of the words. We girls would stand around and watch them. It would be at least four or five boys to us three girls. My one girlfriend was Che-Chee. She stayed in a nice house across the alley from us. She'd come and call to us to come over to her house. The guys would say, "Hambone, hambone where you been? Been to the market and back again". Then they would hit their mouths, then their legs and next I'd get this rhythmic slap and I was to join in on a Hambone rhyme. Then we'd play Hide and Seek and then house. Anyway paws began to make me a pawn at an early age. From kindergarten I'd heard that I was ugly. I knew that I was the object of many a paw. Maybe that's the only way I can be shown affection is by my body being used as a pawn.

Both of my sisters were born while we were living in the rear, or in the alley. Mother and Daddy wanted a boy so bad that my sister was brought home to a blue ruffled bassinet. Sister number two was born. She, also, came home to a blue ruffled bassinet. Daddy and Mother still attempted to have a boy. Mother was disappointed with having another girl. She told us there would be no more babies born to our family. Besides we were getting crowded in these two rooms. You see, the kitchen served as both kitchen and living room. Dad worked as a yardman for the Pennsylvania Railroad Company. It is now known as the Amtrak Railroad Company. The place was oh so crowded. We all grew up there. I had to share my roll away bed with my sisters. We all three slept in the same bed. We would fight at night because we had to share the same bed, the same blankets and the same spread.

The kitchen area was also the bathroom. We had no bathtub fixture in the bathroom. Daddy would heat the water for our bath on top of an old fashion coal stove. The water would be heated in tea kettles or large pots. Water was poured in the tub. We used a round #3 tin tub at first. Mother insisted that we use Ivory soap. Linda and I would have to take baths together. Mother would take old newspapers and place them under and around the bathtub for us to stand on while she dried us. As we grew to at least seven or eight years old Daddy brought an elongated tin bath tub. Then Linda and I took our own baths without mother's assistance. Baths were generally taken on Friday nights. Hair shampoos consisted of Mother drenching our heads with shampoo and drying our hair with large bath towels and combing and parting the hair in sections to dry. A stocking cap made out of Mother's cut off stocking was placed on our heads overnight to dry. The following morning she'd press our hair with a pressing comb and Hair-Rep in a red and black can. When the can looked empty and Mother couldn't place her finger any deeper into the can to obtain extra hair oil, she'd place the can on top of the stove burner to melt the grease. After all, combing through non-permed black hair was very difficult. My scalp was very sensitive. I'd cry while my hair was being straightened. Mother kept us all looking well groomed about our hair.

The same kitchen also served as the washroom. We used the same round #3 tub with a washing board and P & G soap and Colorox to wash dirty clothes. We converted our play area on the porch to a clothes line. We'd also use the yard as a clothes line. Mother would hang the clothes line in at least two rows. The clothes would stay on the line until they'd dry. We'd have to help Mother take them off the line, fold them up and pack them away to iron.

Church members would come by to see how we were doing so they'd say. They'd also come to give us hand-me-down clothing. We were given everything from coats to shoes. It was as if they'd feel sorry for us. Daddy would always save money. He wanted us to move out of those two rooms in the rear of an alley.

Every year during the month of October, St. Louis would have its annual Veiled Prophet Parade. This was the celebration of society through the streets of St. Louis. It so happened that church members knew we lived on the parade route. Our second floor row flat was located behind an office building complex. You entered our house through a gangway or through an alley. I can still see the narrow path of the gangway. It had no sidewalk. It was basically a dirt path with bricks lined up for us to walk on. You had to unlock the little picket fence to get in.

There were ash pits that the business used to dispose of their debris and they'd also throw out cinders or ashes. We'd ramble through the trash and find blank pads to write on. We'd find old ink pens that were being thrown out also. We'd find carbon paper, calendars, adding machine tape paper, paper clips and anything that kids would like to play with to make them feel like grownups. We'd also use the blank pieces of paper to draw on. Daddy and Mother insisted that we do our homework.

The Veiled Prophet Parade was made up of all those big executives who owned those buildings and businesses that surrounded our second row apartment in the alley. What was fun was seeing people that hadn't seen us for one year.

The Veiled Prophet was a rich businessman who wore a mask on his face with a veil with jewels on it. People would line up and wait in anticipation for the parade to begin. We would hear the canon fire to begin the parade. It began at dark. Not one minute before dark. All of the lights along the parade route went out. There were at least forty different floats. All kinds of vendors would be out selling cotton candy, etc. It was similar to floats in the tournament of roses parade. There were bands dispersed between each float. The high school bands and the drill teams felt proud of playing in the VP Parade. Many a parent felt that they had a Miles Davis on their horizon.

One man in particular that belonged to the church would come to the parade each year and would like to put his hands or paws on me and smile. He looked like Santa Claus, dimples and all. He had straight hair, fair skin, and stood about 5'8" tall. His name was as we called him Brother Sims. Mom nor Dad ever knew about him. Paws are for pawning, huh. I didn't like it. After the parade was over, everyone would go home. By it being in October, there'd be a chill in the air! We'd run up the stairs and get in bed.

My hands began to touch my body as I had been touched. Fondling consisted of rubbing the thighs, the outer lips of the vagina and the clitoris. The clitoris was rubbed to the point of my body smelling of itself. Even when no one was around I would feel this sensation. I'd cross my legs and try to squeeze them real tight. Then finally after many days of yearning for him and realizing that I would never see him again I learned how to do what he did. The only bad thing is that the feeling had no certain place or time to hit me. I'd want to touch myself at that time no matter where I was. So, I'd go to the bathroom and rub toilet paper on myself. I tried to feel that way. At other times, I'd wait until I'd go to bed. I'd rub my body against the mattress. Nothing felt as good as the way his hand made me feel. Finally, I touched myself with my own hand.

Finally, mother insisted that we would have to move to larger quarters. She realized that having three daughters meant that each needed privacy. We were told we would be moving. At last the time came. We were told we would be going to a new elementary school. I fell in love with my elementary school. My kindergarten teacher taught my mother. She taught both my sisters. That was special to me.

Finally, the day arrived when we were to move into our new home. I was 10 years old. The interior decorator could not do his job for catching me and throwing himself on my body one hot summer day. This was the first of many days. It was horrible. This man did not know me. He saw me with a sun suit and took advantage of a child. Each day this guy came to our house to do wallpaper, painting and the other things that mother wanted done to the house. Each one of us now had our own bed. Mother saw to it that our room was tastefully decorated. One large bedroom was set up for three young ladies. Our bedspreads all matched. It so happened that the family was out on the day that was the first of many evenings for this interlude with the interior decorator. He was a very trust worthy individual. No parent would be afraid to trust their young pre-teenager with this guy. He would not bother to fondle your daughter. I had on a sun suit that appealed to his appetite obviously. He merely called me to him by asking for a glass of water. Once I brought the water, he drank the first glass then he asked for another glass. While I was pouring the second glass of water his hand touched my buttocks to move over my panties. I remember the fear associated with this episode on my part. I was beginning to develop breasts also. He next began to rub my breast. This hurt so badly I began to cry. He grabbed my panties again and told me not to cry. You see the child is caught between feeing pleasure, pain and fear. If the adult is a trustful individual, he/she has a more easy way of gaining access to the helpless victim. The child's fear gradually is subsided by pleasure. The genitals are massaged until the victim relaxes. Then, as a reward, the child is given money, candy or whatever prevails in the situation. I eventually came to him, for the pain became pleasure. This individual never attempted intercourse. It was fondling that he probably engaged many a child in. I never told my parents. I wonder if anyone ever told their parents.

My next experience was rape. Rape at 16 years old. There was a guy standing one block over from the street I lived on. You see I was new in the neighborhood. Here I was going to the grocery store for my mother. This guy had on an army uniform. He was smoking a cigar. I was certain he was not a threat. After all, he was in uniform. Well, he walked with me to the store. He walked back with me. He asked to come up with him. My newly found girlfriend lived downstairs on the first floor of this row of flats so I said to myself it's all right. After all, he would not try anything because my girlfriend was home. His approach was entirely different. His brother and sister were there in the apartment house but he had his own room. I saw a pointed knife. I was told that I had to go in his room or I would not leave alive. The next thing I did was cooperate. This ugly guy forced me to lie down and he took over. I immediately told my mother of this incident. She went with me in attempts to find this soldier, but our efforts to find him were fruitless that evening. He did reappear. He came to my house. My mother told his he had nothing to say. She advised him of the police report if he did not leave the property immediately he'd be arrested. This nut told my mother that he wanted to marry me. Mother had a fit. He told her he'd take me back in the military with him. He apologized for his behavior. My mother was told that she had a very provocative young daughter. It was then that I was seen as being sexy. I was told that since my parents would not approve of the marriage that I'd have many more encounters. Men shouldn't be held accountable because I had a sexy body.

I was on a date when I was 17 years old with a friend from out of state. At this time, I found fondling fun. After all, I had experienced it so many times without my permission until at this time I was well aware of what was going on. Of course, it was only necking. We were enjoying kissing each other. We were parked in a car in the park in the area called "Lover's Lane". All parks had areas in those days for lovers. The rules were that you weren't to be indulging in any sexual acts. If this happened, you would be jailed for indecent exposure. The policemen always patrolled Lover's Lane. Since you knew what was expected, you acted accordingly. So here we were. The moon was full. The radio was playing "Oh What a Night" by the Dells. The air had such a beautiful clean country smell. There were other lovers parked in the area. While locked in each other's arms, eyes closed, embraced in a kiss we then saw bright lights. We were told to get out of the car. We stood up outside of the car.

Well, these two cops didn't take me that far away or so it seems as I can recall. I had to do what I was told to do. You don't know how scared I was. My knees wouldn't stop shaking. My pretty sundress, my strapless bra, my panties, my slip were all removed by these two rough tons. They told me if I did as told, there would be no problems. I would be returned to my friend in the way that they took me away.

One kept a foolish grin accompanied by loud noises of laughter on him while I followed the other's commands. This went on for at least three hours or so it seemed. My heart felt as if it had ceased beating. I was crying but carrying out each command. I had a blind fold placed over my eyes also. I felt as if I had no insides left at all. Gee, how many girls have been taken away? Was I ever going to see home again? These guys finally decided to order me to get dressed. They were kind enough to give me a towel to wash with. I guess we will be going back to the spot that I was taken from. Praying thank you God, I was taken back to the spot. Could I say thank you God? Most definitely it was awful to experience those events but I was alive. Scared to death and crying, I saw my friend again. I felt so ashamed, I felt that I was to blame.

I've been told on many an occasion that I couldn't be a Social Worker. I drip with sex. I'm so provocative that it interferes with my ability to conceptualize, perceive or use any sense of judgement. I've been told that I don't know what I'm doing. Through networking with a national Social Worker organization, I met a friend in Washington, D.C. at a conference. He is very influential in my life until this day. All I have to do is telephone Dave for any degree of networking. He is a very eligible bachelor indeed. He always says to me "TASHA you and I are going to marry I'm just waiting for you". He'll tell all of us females the same thing. When I call him on the phone I begin by saying Dave, its TASHA let the women go and talk to me for a while. Dave has been a friend indeed. He should really open his own business because he's helped many a professional obtain their current position whatever that may be. It's through Dave that I'm now gainfully employed as both a lecturer and a substance abuse employee counselor in New York City.

The pawning paws didn't cease or lessen in their activity. It so happens that the Studio Villa has plenty of single people living there. We all built a very close and supportive system. We were so close in my building until it became like a college dormitory. We had this one guy that stayed next door to me named Ben. Ben worked as an accountant. He played football in college. That's how he obtained his M.B.A. Then my across-the-hall neighbor was Brenda. Brenda is a civil engineer. She is a very pretty lady who looked at me and my neighbor Jannie who wore dresses to work and resented the fact that she had to dress in coveralls. Ben would keep a bunch of his frat brothers at his place each weekend. His friends were wild. They'd all do whatever alcohol/fun drug they wanted because they had plenty for everyone. There was plenty of liquor and food also. One thing interesting about Ben. He was big, but neat and clean. He couldn't help that his friends were combining the purpose of their visit. They came and spent many hours looking at his cable system (Home Box Office and Showtime) or his video camera receiver. You know what videos were shown "Vanessa Del" and whoever were considered the porn king and queen. We respected each other very much. Of course, Ben wanted to introduce us to his frat brothers who would visit him from California, Florida and Hawaii. It didn't matter to him because his personality was so adorable. Jacques often commented about our closeness and concern for each other.

Winter was wild. It was cold. Here I was prohibited from being gainfully employed in New Jersey or New York. After all, to refresh your memory, I'd been black balled from working on the East coast. Mr. West had told me to relocate to Florida and not continue the pursuit of my case of discrimination/harassment due to sex against him. Well, I felt as if I had a right as a citizen of American to reside wherever I wanted to reside. This meant that I was going to stay here and work. The temperature dropped to 10 below that year. We had many snowstorms. I can remember how the ice blew up against my face, the wind hollered as it's snow felt like razor blades on my nose and cheeks. I thought the commute would be more enjoyable. It was so cold until the ritual of getting dressed wasn't fun anymore. I'd have to put on my thermal undies. Ladies thermal had become a necessary item in my winter wardrobe. I looked for real pretty sets.

There was a large selection of sets with rose buds in different color and both short and long sleeves or both short and long legs. I'd buy my sets to match my bras and underslips. I had to remain totally matched and feminine to myself. I purchased a down filled coat a couple of years earlier. It had a hood on it for extra warmth to my head. As a matter of fact, it was purchased right before going into the hospital for the dental corrective surgery. I didn't want to catch a head cold at that time either. I wore leg warmers that matched my hat, scarf and gloves. Believe me I'd do anything to avoid the various viruses that hit the area each winter. I'd learned to ride the subways thanks to my co-workers and Jacques. We'd often meet each other for dates on the New York Transit Subway system. No matter how cold we'd brave it and meet each other. Your nose felt as if it didn't belong to you anymore. Your fingers were ice. You couldn't move them because they were frozen. One would feel as if they were on ice skate because the streets were glazed with ice. The snow would fall and pile up on top of the ice. We actually experienced three snow storms in one week. I'd pray each night after arriving in from the cold. I'd have to walk in the street where the cars were driving because at least there was a path to walk on that was clear. I began to know Stuyvesant by the street pavement. How many more days of this frigid weather would we have to endure God? I'd both pray prayers of thanks and question God in the same prayer.

We on Stuyvesant, would band together and buy or cook food. We'd invite each other over. Ben, Brenda, Jannie and me made the foursome of the third floor. Jannie would go to church each and every Sunday. Although we'd stay up to 3:00-4:00 AM amidst those winter storms, she'd still go to church with her sisters. I'd notice how close she and her sisters were. I couldn't help but reflect upon the great division to the point of actual dislike or hatred that existed between me and my sisters. It was as if we never knew each other anymore. Whatever the problem was will never be resolved because they never wanted to work at resolution. I was very ugly with the teeth that protruded. I corrected it because it was a complex to me. I married and raised my son. They actually attempt poison or turn my son against me also. I refused to allow men that were willing to paw over me as an adult to do so. I refuse to lay with men in front of my child. I choose to marry rather than live-with, My values have always been different. I am secure in my being. I use my head and not my tail.

Paws are for touching, huh? My tail is my tail. So, it's nice. You think so. I'm sexy, I'd seductive, and I'm provocative? I have a sexy tail. Tails have tales to tell. I'm telling you the tale as it should be told. All Social Workers have many tales to tell. This Social Worker is trying to tell you her tale. She isn't a seductive woman from her point of view. She can't stop others from viewing her tail from their vantage point. She sees their tails, or is it tales also. I'd like to say that I'm not accustomed nor will I tolerate the pawning paws that I've had to let pawn over me as a child. I am a professional woman. I am a lecturer, I am a counselor, and I am a Social Worker with a tale to tell. All in all, I've told a story/tale that has been a mixture of good and bad situations. Of course, the good outweighs the bad.

You can change your life no matter what the circumstances. My new look (the corrective dental surgery) has given me a second chance in life. Just because I had one child as a teenager didn't mean that I had to have three. It didn't mean that I became a welfare mother, or a high school drop-out. I didn't quit. I was determined to work and someday marry and give my child a home. I'm hoping that all of you single young mothers will find encouragement and realize your goals can be achieved. I'm telling all persons both professional and non-professional to expose sexual harassment in whatever form. So you'll have to suffer humiliation if you don't expose it. Damned if you do and damned if you don't. You're in a double-bind situation. Expose sexual harassment in the work place. If you don't find a means of support by either your family, your friends or your church, you will feel that you can't cope. God is my support. As I look back and think, I don't know how I survived. God was my bridge, he carried me over the bad times, the troubled waters, the stormy weather. I possess sensibility, sensitivity and sensuousness.

Often times, I felt that I was a pawn at work, as a young child, and in my interpersonal relationships. Have you ever felt that the Social Worker shouldn't have to take time to see a psycho-therapist? After all, during earlier experiences in life I'd rejected psychotherapy. Believe me, I'd almost hit rock bottom. In attempting to remain afloat I'd been evicted almost, two years in a row I'd been referred to Landlord-Tenant Court. I felt that I had no one to ask for help. Was I having trouble with men? I don't know what to do. I didn't know who to trust. Finally, I started to feel as if I needed God, and psychotherapy. This man was truly a fantastic psychologist. He could make sexually abused children open up to him. It was something in his face that would make you feel as if it was ok to tell him. He has a fantastic secretary also. She would do the initial contact. Her hospitality made you feel at home in this town who had gotten known for its hostility towards non-residents. I lived in Irvington, New Jersey not Maplewood. He had brown eyes and drove a black sports car. He treated everyone as equals. Actually I was afraid that he'd do what everyone else had done. It was so difficult for me to be the one who was receiving instead of giving the therapy. Dr. Moore was tall. He stood at least six foot. He dressed in a very relaxed fashion. He never wore a two piece suit. Since I had just recently lost my job as a result of the sexual harassment I had experienced at the health center I felt like Dr. Moore had already classified me as Schizophrenic. He assured me that he hadn't given me a category or a label. I told him how my previous supervisor had decided to be an animal and destroy my life and my career but he told me that he had experienced similar kinds of craziness. He'd say to me "TASHA" you're going to have to think about becoming self-reliant. He encouraged me to talk about why I found it so difficult to talk about something that obviously hurt and was still hurting me badly. I'd begin to cry. I still wouldn't talk about it. How could I tell him how many men had felt as if I was their pawn? How could I tell him how manyencounters I'd had with lesbians? Everyone had begun to say that I was seductive.

I didn't know how to accept myself. I was hurt although I'd begun enjoying the best of both worlds. On one hand I was dating Jacques. Jacques was 16 years younger than me. He is fine. I spoke in many sessions to Dr. Moore about Jacques. We had so many beautiful times. We'd ride the subway line together. We'd go to the Bronx Zoo together. We'd dance together all night long non-stop. We'd say to each other your place or mine. Dr. Moore encouraged me to enjoy myself. He'd say don't restrict yourself. But what if all Jacques wants is my body? Suppose I'm his pawn? I like his paws though. His paws were welcomed anytime. Anytime it was whenever we spent weekends together. We often spoke about the many years of age difference between us. It so happened that both of us were born in May. We had similar interests. We both enjoyed theatre, good music. We'd gone to various jazz shows together. At times due to his job as an accountant with a large industrial facility in Long Island he'd be given job assignments out of town. He had also purchased a co-op. He was very stable. I didn't choose him because he was young. As I mentioned before I met Jacques at Buppies in East Orange, New Jersey. What attracted me to him was his ability to speak well. He was very knowledgeable. I was taught early by Mother to know what you're talking about when you open your mouth. At least this was the picture Jacques presented. We exchanged business cards. On the back of our cards we wrote our home telephone numbers. I thought Jacques was dressed very appropriate for a Sunday afternoon affair of singles meeting singles. We sat at the bar and talked about our background. Where are you from? Are you a native New Yorker? How about us planning to meet each other this weekend for dinner and a movie? He had such a beautiful smile and his personality was so alive. TASHA what does this guy want? TASHA slow down. He's only after your tail. Can't you remember how you've been told how you walk? Can't you remember being called Miss Prick Teaser? Well, what are you going to do? Are you going to let fear take over your life?

Then there's the guy who I'd been looking at for at least two years. He was so fine. He was so distinguished. I had to really do my homework to find out about him. Was he single? I know who he is. How can I tactfully get his attention? He's definitely good looking. He's got so many women who are more eligible than me. They are first of all financially stable, professional stable, and pretty. It's so hard out here competing to get one of the most eligible bachelors. What is it that I want from Tom? Tom makes me want him so that the chemical reaction makes me break out in a sweat on my forehead when I see or think I'm going to see him. I began to react as a teenager all over again. It so happens that I've told him how I feel about men who are merely out for sexual favors. He has often merely looked at me and given me a smile. I love his one inch gray spot in the top of his forehead. Would I resist his advancements or his pawning paws? I'd have to answer that the encounter would be mutually acceptable to both parties. Tom is the type of guy that everyone loves. Both men and women know that he is one that many an individual depends upon. He is very active with educational organizations for both minority and indigent individuals. When I see a male that I'm interested in, then I do the pursuing. Sometimes I have to change my activities and lessen them in my pursuits. Would I be the one to do the pawing? I'll let you think about the previous chapters that you've read about me. Again, I'm a very sensible and sensuous individual. There is no way that I'd attempt to seduce Tom. There's no need for me to try it. I'm very direct. I'm so direct in my approach that people or Tom might have taken it in a negative manner. Tom dresses like Mr. Conservative America which makes me think he lacks nothing in his wardrobe. I first noticed him in the winter time. He wore a beige wool trench coat. His clothes are tailored to his body. We rode an elevator together. I looked at him and he looked at me. We were finally introduced. His handshake was so firm and warm. He has a unique way of looking at you directly in the eye. This was what fascinated me. How could he be so direct, warm and hospitable? Gee, if I could get to know him. Yes, I was aware of the women. Sometimes there are so many facets to one individual that are intriguing to you, or to me until I knew that I wanted to know one of the facets. Oh, not the tail. Oh, nor do I want to paw him. Am I sexually attracted to him?

Tom is a man whom I'll probably never ever have. For one thing he won't permit it. If I look at the acceptable age difference I'd say we are perfect. I'd have to do some readjustments in my behavior. For example, I'd have to become more stable in as far as securing a job is concerned. Starting all over in a career places me at a financial disadvantage. I'll always desire and want to have Tom around me as my friend. At least with him I can be me. He accepts me. One thing he does, he reminds me that he's not ready for a serious relationship. Tom stays my friend. Allow me to be in love with you for who you are and what you've done for me.

Many women can't look at themselves and smile. Many women can look at themselves and smile and feel good about their achievements. I have only one regret that my sisters and I will never be able to enjoy our true relationship. This is another tale that needs to be told. I have no regrets about the profession that I've chosen. I love the job that I do. I chose the career because I wanted to help other young mothers. If it hadn't been for those Social Workers who looked at me as a young teenage mother with a child I don't know where I'd be today. My child was a very loveable baby. He had a way of winning people's hearts. He was cheerful. He loved to hug and kiss people. He was fat and had curly hair all over his head. I knew I couldn't have two children. I was taught about condoms, intra-uterine devices and birth control pills. These were relatively new devices back in the early 60's. A Social Worker sat with me and told me about family planning and birth control. Being a secretary wouldn't take care of me and my child. It wasn't enough income to sustain us in any decent lifestyle. The same problems exist today some 30 years later as existed then. The same job still has to be performed. Someone has to continue to be the helping professional. This fictional tale is not to put down any Social Worker. It is merely the tale of one Social Worker names Tasha. It merely attempts to show how Tasha was a pawn to many paws. It showed that she was highly misunderstood because many wanted to crush her spirit because she didn't conform to their lifestyle. In the same instance, they wanted to be like her. This is the end to TAILS OF A SOCIAL WORKER.

TASHA

REFLECTIONS

TASHA watched the midnight rain – her past staring back from the windowpane.
Still hanging tough with an iron will – still bearing scars that will never heal.

TASHA.
A symbol of struggle and pride; forever unyielding in her fight to survive.
Doing the best one can do – is nothing to do with what's expected of you.

TASHA still daring to take a stand. TASHA still doing the best she can – the system would make it easier if she were a man. You all know the tale.
No matter how it's told, to succeed in the patronage game – you've got to sell your soul.

With love,

Written by
Cruz